ONE ON ONE

PLAYING WITH A PURPOSE

ONE ON ONE

PLAYING WITH A PURPOSE

MONOLOGUES FOR KIDS AGES 7–15

EDITED BY BOB SHUMAN AND STEPHEN FIFE
WITH CONTRIBUTING EDITORS
MARIT SHUMAN AND ELOISE ROLLINS-FIFE

An Imprint of Hal Leonard Corporation
New York

Published in 2013 by Applause Theatre & Cinema Books

An Imprint of Hal Leonard Corporation
7777 West Bluemound Road
Milwaukee, WI 53213

Trade Book Division Editorial Offices
33 Plymouth St., Montclair, NJ 07042

Printed in the United States of America

Book design by Kristina Rolander

Library of Congress Cataloging-in-Publication Data

One on one : playing with a purpose : monologues for kids ages 7-15 / edited by Bob Shuman and Stephen Fife ; with Marit E. Shuman and Eloise Rollins-Fife.
pages cm
Includes bibliographical references and index.
ISBN 978-1-55783-841-4 (pbk. : alk. paper)
1. Monologues--Juvenile literature. 2. Acting--Auditions--Juvenile literature. 3. Children's writings, American. 4. Children--Drama. 5. Teenagers--Drama. I. Shuman, Bob. II. Fife, Stephen. III. Shuman, Marit E. IV. Rollins-Fife, Eloise.
PN2080.O557 2013
808.82'45--dc23

2012050428

ISBN 978-1-55783-841-4

www.applausebooks.com

CONTENTS

PART TWO: MONOLOGUES FOR BOYS

PART THREE: MONOLOGUES BY STUDENTS

INTRODUCTION

We tiptoed through the ancient Greeks and rifled through Shakespeare in an ever-widening circle: from Iphigenia to Ophelia, Puck to Peter Pan—and even...Edith Ann. Actually, the stacks of the play collection at the Lincoln Center Library, in New York City, were pillaged, backward (it just seemed easier to start at the end of the alphabet). Concurrently, we talked to contemporary dramatists who write for and work with young actors, like Stephen Fife (one of our editors) and Crystal Skillman and Dylan Dawson (who were scribing for the 52nd Street Project in Hell's Kitchen, helping to create miniplays based on individual interests and talents). Anything to find the best nonmusical parts possible for ages 7 to 15—the best roles available celebrating *you*.

We contacted agents and publishers of Pulitzer Prize winners like Nilo Cruz, Frances Goodrich and Albert Hackett, Lorraine Hansberry, Quiara Alegría Hudes, Donald Margulies, Lanford Wilson, and Paul Zindel. Charming and gracious as they were, we wanted more. Yes, doors slammed in our faces, calls were not returned, e-mails became terse or languished—but always, always, someone or something redeemed us, making the project stronger. We heard from the representatives of writers best known for comedy, such as Lily Tomlin and Jane Wagner, as well as those of Carrie Hamilton and Carol Burnett (although their piece in this book isn't comedic). We put ads on blogs and in newsletters. We asked for material from writers we knew, writers we'd heard about, and writers who thought we must be kidding.

On a commuter bus, youth director Kim Johnson offered to let us read monologues that she used with her students in New York City and had collected over the years: they were like gold. The question was apparent: Why couldn't these be found in bookstores, all neatly in *one* place? Ingenious directors, teachers, and parents had put youth theatre together in their communities, passing strong speeches along and compiling notebooks, but core work was scattered everywhere.

Monologues, those delicate objects of passion, anger, heartbreak, and whimsy, are like the theatre itself, existing in the present moment, and can become unobtainable because of rights issues or mere neglect. Beautiful pieces from the past can be shelved or lost as new work, new plays, new artists take their places. Reclaiming this material was part of our task, much like locating forgotten folk- or fairytales or finding melodies heard long ago.

Becoming more international in our search, we gathered selections from Belgium, Canada, Great Britain, Greece, Guyana, Ireland, and Spain, as well as writing from realists like Carson McCullers, even magical realists like José Rivera. We delved into pieces from Israel Horovitz and Herb Gardner, Lisa Loomer and Caridad Svich, and those based on famous fiction, like Robert Louis Stevenson's *Treasure Island* as dramatized by Ken Ludwig, and Roald Dahl's *Danny the Champion of the World* adapted by David Wood. We also decided to go straight to original sources, the words of Lewis Carroll, Miguel de Cervantes, James Joyce (one of his novels is represented, as well as a nugget from his sole play), and Mark Twain. Thanks to Tracy Cho and Steve Fife, we were then introduced to outstanding monologues by middle school students in the Los Angeles public school system who had been working with theatre artists from the Center Theatre Group.

As editor, director, actress, and acting teacher Joyce Henry maintained, performers want characters who can *move* them–even if they need to be presented in a class or audition…tomorrow, for composing on their own, writers search for models. We began considering and highlighting various styles from Shakespeare to Ibsen, Naomi Wallace to Jean-Rock Gaudreault—from across the ages, beyond New York, and above cultural politics to encourage… possibilities.

The best way, actually, to get to know characters is by reading the original plays they're in (if they can't be found on the Web or in a bookstore, you can find them by looking at the author and agent permissions information at the end of this anthology so you can make inquiries; do make your best efforts). Monologues, of course, can also be written just to be monologues, and such examples are included here, too.

In the table of contents, we have noted that Edith Ann is 6; Peter Pan can be 7 years or even 7 days old. In *Arcadia*, Thomasina Coverly is age 13 years and 10 months, and in *The Member of the Wedding* Frankie is 1/6 shy of 13 years old. Having such knowledge can help give clues to character, to use as part of an actor's investigation. We are not implying that "part-takers" or "theatrians" (Elizabethan terms) need be exactly those ages to play the roles. We just wanted to offer as much information as possible. With a few exceptions, the words and actions of others involved in a scene are also presented—as indicated in the playwright's original script–and have been placed in brackets. This material, which may not be of immediate importance to the performance at hand, likewise, gives a fuller understanding of the character and the situation being portrayed. It might even necessitate new, imaginative physical action.

During different periods of history, characters can be thought of differently. Iphigenia, Antigone, Juliet, and Ophelia, as part of their cultures, did not question marrying early, whereas today, in the U.S., someone would need to be around 18 or in China, 22. The Boy in *Henry V* follows a war to France in 1415, serving soldiers he dislikes. Yet, he's probably in his early- to mid-teens. The contemporary playwright Craig Wright thought to have heroes and gods played by young actors—actually girls, although boys can play the roles, too. Homer, a poet, wouldn't have considered such a notion when he, believed to be blind or even more than one person, recited passages regarding Achilles and Priam. Juliet and Ophelia, even in Shakespeare's time, would not have been played by girls, although boys' companies became fashionable in London during the Elizabethan and Jacobean eras. As cited in *Hamlet*, in the 1600s, their popularity sent grownup actors to tour on the road.

Mark Twain actually let Huckleberry Finn—as he is traveling down the Mississippi River in the 1800s—perform a bad version of one of the soliloquies from *Hamlet* (the Prince of Denmark is usually thought to be around age 30; Huck is about 13). If it is done with imagination and an understanding of character, just about anyone can play any role. All young actors can play Sam in Kayla Cagan's "Dog People" or Carlos in Carol S. Lashof's "The Underprivileged Club" as well as many more in this volume. We have noticed that, at this point, theatre literature seems to include fewer minority voices and more monologues about the experiences of girls than of boys, and we look forward to the day when such imbalances will be corrected. We're also hoping that professional playwrights will decide to present more positive portrayals of young people in their dramatic writing. Why shouldn't creative work be free and daring, thrilling and interesting for all ages?

And here's some advice to all performers: Remember to stay relaxed, and don't forget to breathe! It may also be appropriate to make eye contact with the audience from time to time as well as to use a prop that helps bring the scene to life. When writing or acting, be aware of and incorporate physical action. Let teachers and directors, family and friends, see talent, originality, and ability—we want to appreciate important work (new or classic), whether a "player" or "stage-walker" (other Elizabethan terms told to us by scholar Ian Donaldson) is 8 or 80. People are becoming increasingly aware of this burgeoning world of youth theatre, so let our voices be sung! Young people really are all of our futures, so, take your time and put some effort into preparation. Make these characters real and they will become friends—not just in a rehearsal space and in this magical world called theatre; they will be friends anywhere, and for life.

THE EDITORS

PART ONE

MONOLOGUES FOR GIRLS

AMY'S SUPER-AMAZING INCREDIBLE MAKEOVER

BY ELOISE ROLLINS-FIFE AND STEPHEN FIFE

AMY, *a smart girl in her early teens, is standing in front of a mirror, near a pile of makeup that isn't hers.* SHE *is trying to apply cosmetics to become popular and get a date for the dance, but* SHE *lacks experience and can't seem to get it right.* SHE *talks to herself in the mirror as* SHE *tries to figure out what to do.* (NOTE TO ACTOR: ONLY PRETEND TO PUT ON MAKEUP.)

SCENE

AMY*'s bathroom, looking into the mirror. Makeup is on a nearby table.*

TIME

The present.

AMY: Okay, so this shouldn't be too hard. I mean, I looked through all the teen mags, and here are the makeup thingies they said to use. The makeup "containers," I guess. Or "tins." Or— Oh, who cares, Amy! Stop obsessing about words! That's what got us into this mess in the first place. This "dating crisis." This "life without boys." This— Oh, just stop it, Amy! Stop it. Concentrate on putting on makeup. Focus on becoming popular. Getting a date for the dance. Yes, if I can just get this right, then I'm sure my life will change. Transform. Revamp. Zip it! Just zip it! Or "keep your trap shut." Or—

(SHE *stops her word play, starts putting on blush.*)

Maybe if I just put a little more right here, then I'll be known as "the cool, pretty girl," not "the human dictionary"…or…oh, no! Crap, I look like a clown! (SHE *furiously rubs at her cheeks to get the blush off.*) Or a fool. Or a joker. Stop it, Amy! Just stop! (SHE *stops rubbing her face.*) I don't understand! How do millions of girls do this? Girls who can't tie my shoelaces when it comes to studying, girls who ask for my help with their essays, girls who— (SHE *has removed the blush.* SHE *smiles at herself in the mirror, stops.*) "Can't tie my shoelaces"? What does that even mean? They know how to tie shoelaces. And they know how to put on makeup, too. It comes as easily to them as making small talk with boys. Something I also can't do.

(SHE *starts putting on blush again, more carefully this time.*)

I certainly can't show up to school with just chapstick on anymore, right? But maybe girls who win the science fair and are in the honors program just aren't meant to be popular. (SHE *stops, makes faces at herself—an ugly one, silly one, and so on.*) Oh, who am I kidding? No matter how much mascara I wear, I'll never be one of them. So what if my lipstick is always the wrong color and my shoes are always a few seasons behind, and my blush is always smudged? There's just not enough concealer in the world to make me look cool.

(SHE *rubs off the makeup again—but now* SHE*'s not angry or upset anymore.*)

I can't wait until this is all over. When I'm in college maybe I'll finally be popular. Or maybe the real world is just like middle school, and I'll never fit in. Either way, I'm never putting on… (SHE *reads the label of blush.*) "sugarcane blush" ever again. (SHE *tosses all the makeup in the trash can and looks in the mirror.*) How can a sugarcane "blush" anyway? Oh, maybe if a boy sugarcane says something bad. (SHE *laughs at her own joke, turns to leave.*) Or naughty. Or wicked. Or…

ANTIGONE
BY SOPHOCLES

ANTIGONE, *at least 14-15, daughter of Oedipus, has defied her uncle, King Creon, and buried her brother Polyneices, despite the fact that he was an enemy of the state. Before* SHE *is taken to her death, for this is her punishment,* SHE *explains that* SHE *believes her course of action was correct.*

SCENE
In front of the Theban palace in ancient Greece. Harsh sun.

TIME
Noon.

ANTIGONE: O tomb, O marriage-chamber, hollowed out
House that will watch forever, where I go.
To my own people, who are mostly there;
Persephone has taken them to her.
Last of them all, ill-fated past the rest,
Shall I descend, before my course is run.
Still when I get there I may hope to find
I come as a dear friend to my dear father,
To you, my mother, and my brother, too.
All three of you have known my hand in death.
I washed your bodies, dressed them for the grave,
Poured out the last libation at the tomb.

Last, Polyneices knows the price I pay
For doing final service to his corpse.
And yet the wise will know my choice was right.
Had I had children or their father dead,
I'd let them moulder. I should not have chosen
In such a case to cross the state's decree.
What is the law that lies behind these words?
One husband gone, I might have found another,
Or a child from a new man in first child's place,
But with my parents hid away in death,
No brother, ever, could spring up for me.
Such was the law by which I honored you.
But Creon thought the doing was a crime,
A dreadful daring, brother of my heart.
So now he takes and leads me out by force.
No marriage-bed, no marriage-song for me,
And since no wedding, so no child to rear.
I go, without a friend, struck down by fate,
Live to the hollow chambers of the dead.
What divine justice have I disobeyed?
Why, in my misery, look to the gods for help?
Can I call any of them my ally?
I stand convicted of impiety,
The evidence my pious duty done.
Should the gods think that this is righteousness,
In suffering I'll see my error clear.
But if it is the others who are wrong
I wish them no greater punishment than mine.

ARCADIA
BY TOM STOPPARD

THOMASINA COVERLY, *13 years and 10 months, is an English mathematical and scientific genius.* SHE *has been translating Latin poetry, written by the poet Lord Byron, for her tutor, Septimus Hodge, before the scene begins. Outside of class, love and poetry are issues of concern, and the grounds, where the play is set, are being redesigned to show a new taste for gothic, as opposed to classical style.*

SCENE
A bare schoolroom on the garden front of a stately home in Derbyshire, England. A large table occupies the center with straight-backed chairs and a reading stand.

TIME
April 11, 1809.

THOMASINA: Mama is in love with Lord Byron.

[SEPTIMUS: (*Absorbed.*) Yes. Nonsense.]

THOMASINA: It is not nonsense. I saw them together in the gazebo.

[(*Septimus's pen stops moving; he raises his eyes to her at last.*)]

Lord Byron was reading to her from his satire, and mama was laughing, with her head in her best position.

[SEPTIMUS: She did not understand the satire, and was showing politeness to a guest.]

THOMASINA: She is vexed with papa for his determination to alter the park, but that alone cannot account for her politeness to a guest. She came downstairs hours before her custom. Lord Byron was amusing at breakfast. He paid you a tribute, Septimus.

[SEPTIMUS: Did he?]

THOMASINA: He said you were a witty fellow, and he had almost by heart an article you wrote about—well, I forget what, but it concerned a book called *The Maid of Turkey* and how you would not give it to your dog for dinner.

[SEPTIMUS: Ah. Mr. Chater was at breakfast, of course.]

THOMASINA: He was, not like certain lazybones.

[SEPTIMUS: He does not have Latin to set and mathematics to correct.

(*He takes* THOMASINA*'s lesson book from underneath Plautus and tosses it down the table to her.*)]

THOMASINA: Correct? What was incorrect in it? (SHE *looks into the book.*) Alpha minus? Pooh!

What is the minus for?

[SEPTIMUS: For doing more than was asked.]

THOMASINA: You did not like my discovery?

[SEPTIMUS: A fancy is not a discovery.]

THOMASINA: A gibe is not a rebuttal.

[(*Septimus finishes what he is writing. He folds the pages into a letter. He has sealing wax and the means to melt it. He seals the letter and writes on the cover. Meanwhile—*)]

You are churlish with me because mama is paying attention to your friend. Well, let them elope, they cannot turn back the advancement of knowledge. I think it is an excellent discovery. Each week I plot your equations dot for dot, *xs* against *ys* in all manner of algebraical relation, and every week they draw themselves as commonplace geometry, as if the world of forms were nothing but arcs and angles. God's truth, Septimus, if there is an equation for a curve like a bell, there must be an equation for one like a bluebell, and if a bluebell, why not a rose? Do we believe nature is written in numbers?

[SEPTIMUS: We do.]

THOMASINA: Then why do your equations only describe the shapes of manufacture?

[SEPTIMUS: I do not know.]

THOMASINA: Armed thus, God could only make a cabinet.

[SEPTIMUS: He has mastery of equations which lead into infinities where we cannot follow.]

THOMASINA: What a faint-heart! We must work outward from the middle of the maze. We will start with something simple. (SHE *picks up tile apple leaf.*) I will plot this leaf and deduce its equation. You will be famous for being my tutor when Lord Byron is dead and forgotten.

ARIA FOR A SAXOPHONE

BY MARIT E. SHUMAN

ARIA, *14, is lying in her sleeping bag, cranking a LED flashlight, which becomes brighter and brighter as the scene progresses.* SHE *is on a three-day school camping trip before the start of ninth grade and has been talking to a Young Saxophone Player for several hours.*

SCENE

A camp-out in upstate New York.

TIME

In the middle of the night at the end of summer.

ARIA: (*Lying on her stomach in a sleeping bag.*) Why is it easier to say things in the darkness, whispering, than face to face?

I stayed outside tonight because I didn't want to sleep in a tent that smelled like bug spray and that still, funny enough, had that one annoying mosquito in it. And, because of that, in the past five hours, we've basically hit the fast-forward button on… friendship. It's like POW, here's what's happened to me in the past fourteen years, and you're gonna have a quiz on it tomorrow. (*Sits up.*)

Maybe it's the dark. Things are different...like dreams, and the truth. You can't see anything, and I guess then you don't believe anything....What I mean is, there are no consequences in the dark, everything you say you can deny, pass off as a vivid dream... or the result of a sleep-deprived mind...playing tricks on you. (*Pause.*)

...You know?! They're too unformed: Dreams. Too shadowy to be seen in the light...too fragile to be judged there. I don't know....(*Pause.*) It's always in the dark, though. You dream in the dark, your subconscious is allowed to...for a short amount of time, to be put above the conscious. Rule the conscious. Do you know what I'm saying?

(*Reaching out in front of her.*) Where are you? Where's your face? Is that you? (*Pause.*)

You should have seen it today, your face, when you were playing the saxophone. Pure feeling...the sax is the most emotional of all instruments. No, that's not what I mean. Not the saxophone itself, but...have you ever watched the musicians in the orchestra? The actors are going crazy on stage trying to portray all of these scripted emotions: love, hate, love-hate. But, in the pit, the feelings are actually taking place. It's like the music strips away all of the...I don't know, all the layers of defense...

...Everything just seems much more...so much...real-er out here. It's like being at the Grand Canyon or Niagara Falls or someplace like that. The stars are brighter. Maybe it's just that the sky is so dark. (*Pause.*)

I think this will end though...since we're being honest. I've told you everything, my...yes, everything is the word. Tomorrow, I'll roll up my sleeping bag and politely talk to you at breakfast. And in the next week or two we'll say hello and make some inane chit-chat. But in three months, I'll ignore you and you'll do the same to me. It won't be rude, just practical. I'll be the bubbly, friendly, Miss Best All Around, studying 24/7 to get a scholarship to Yale—and you, the brooding musician, will end up down in the village playing sonatas in some hole-in-the-wall café.

When we wake up tomorrow there'll be nothing left to say. (*The flashlight is now completely on.* SHE *hands it to him as* SHE *gets up to leave.*)

Here's your flashlight.

BLACK SHEEP

BY BARA SWAIN

LORI, *in her early teens, has mixed feelings about having a newborn brother until a chance encounter with a family friend gives her a different perspective.*

SCENE

A hospital lobby.

TIME

Morning.

LORI: (*Eats Good & Plenty candy while telling this.*) My mom gave birth to my little brother last night. It's pretty embarrassing—her being forty years old, I mean. Anyway, I visited him in the hospital at 11:30 last night. And it's weird, you know, because for the rest of my life, I'll always be fourteen years older than Harold. (SHE *rolls her eyes.*) Yeah, do you believe that name? They named him after my Great Uncle Harry—and Mom said that Harold will always look up to me. Who's she kidding—look up to me! Me, the "black sheep" of the family! Everyone knows that my sister, Jean, is their little darling, with the perfect attendance record and the perfect hair and a perfect SAT score in math. Jean started college in September, so now it's just me and…and Great Uncle Harry's namesake. Anyway, I think my mom meant that Harold will—literally—look up to me because I'm, like, fifty inches taller than he is and three inches taller than my older sister. (*After a moment.*)

So after some gootchie gootchie gooing last night and watching two diaper changes, I got kind of bored and walked to the nurse's station, when, what do you know, I heard someone calling my name! Crazy, huh? I looked around, and it was my sister's friend Lisa, who is the late-shift medical photographer at the hospital. She invited me to come back to her office, which was just down the corridor from the emergency room, between the main waiting room and the pay phones. It was the size of a broom closet or a bathroom stall, only it smelled like black licorice.

Lisa was there, cramming a licorice stick down her throat. She looked up and waved. "You know what twizzlers are made of?" I told her. "The same thing as plastic straws. It takes, like, six years to digest licorice." Lisa's like an aspiring photojournalist, and on some nights she and her instamatic roam the floors, snapping shots—mostly in the surgical intensive care and burn units. As soon as I sat down, she said, "It's quiet tonight. Wanna look at my new stuff?" So my sister's friend opened her photo album and a box of Good & Plenty (LORI *holds up her candy box.*), then turned to the last page. And, holy moly! I swear, an 11-fingered baby screamed at the lens—like me and Jean did when we watched an old horror film with Bruce Willis…(LORI *imitates Haley Joel Osment.*) *"I see dead people."* (LORI *shivers.*) And next, there was an arm, broken in, like, four places. And then a print of a French-pedicured toe, black with gangrene. And suddenly—I thought about Harold.

My little brother, Harold. I saw his little tiny toe all black with gangrene. Hey! No way I'm going to let him end up on a page in Lisa's album. I mean, there was only so much I could do to protect him, but…it took me under five minutes to get back to my mom's room. I was just in time to see Harold's face turn red, then blue, and then he let out a blood-curdling scream. I picked him up, counted his fingers, and rubbed his back. What else should I do? I'm his big sister now.

BOOTS

BY CONNIE SCHINDEWOLF

MARLEY, *a girl who is entering seventh grade, knows that wearing boots and a coat in Florida in the summer doesn't seem to make much sense, but* SHE *has her reasons.*

SCENE
Bradenton, Florida.

TIME
In late August.

MARLEY: (SHE *sits on a bus bench, takes off her sneakers and takes a pair of boots out of her backpack, stuffs her sneakers into it, starts to put on the boots.*) So, I'm walking out the door on the first day of school with my new boots on, and my mom starts laughing. She says, "Marley, do you think it's going to snow or something? We live in Florida, and it's August and it's supposed to be eighty-seven degrees today! Are you crazy?" I explained how I had to wear something new. I was careful to keep my jacket buttoned up so she wouldn't see how much of my chest would be bare without it. She just kept laughing and saying my feet and legs were going to sweat to death, and I had to take them off.

Great! Way to ruin my first day of seventh grade, Mom! I mean it's already stressful enough not knowing who is going to be in your first period and if you're going to have lunch with your best friends! (SHE *finishes putting on her first boot, starts putting on the second.*) But I know the answer for next year. I saw them on this girl named Izzy last week, they were the coolest boots! They were purple and as high and as faux-furry as mine, but then the feet turned into purple flip-flops! It was so cool! That's what I'm getting for next year cuz Mom was righ— (SHE *finishes putting on the second boot, stands up.*) My feet are HOT, HOT, HOT in these! Yeah. So next year the flip-flop boots for me. My mom will embarrass me, I know, and call them thong boots or something like that. She just doesn't know what she does to my life! Yep, next year first day...flip-flop boots and a new low cut top to show off my chest...maybe I'll even have something to show off by then! (*Looks up like praying.*) Please?

CITY IN A STRAIT

BY OYAMO

ALEXANDRA, *13-14, tells about the day her best friend stopped being one.*

SCENE

The bustling streets of the city.

TIME

Now.

ALEXANDRA: Alexandra Macon here. Sandra and I were best friends, we played together constantly, studied together in school, walked home together, giggling and telling each other secrets. She was a white girl. Our parents didn't allow us to go into each other's house. My mama would fix Sandra a plate, I had to go in and get it for her. She'd gobble it down. Never told her mother how she ate on our porch with me lots of times. I wouldn't eat nothing from her house. Her mama was nasty, fingernails dirty, hair looks wet with wax or something, eyes all red. Somewhere around the time we turned twelve, she stopped playing with me, stopped talking, everything. Just chopped off whatever it was that made us good friends. Never saw her again.

DAD

BY CHRISTINA LINHARDT

ERIN, *a girl in her early teens, has been looking after her sick father for years, and it's tearing her apart.* SHE *wants to be a good daughter, but* SHE *also needs to have her own life. What can* SHE *do?*

SCENE

At home, outside her dad's room.

TIME

Evening.

ERIN: (SHE *is doing her homework at a table, looks up.*) What can I say anymore? It's always about him. Always. Everything is. I mean—I know how that sounds. He's sick. It's not his fault. But it's been going on for more than three years now, and that's a long time. And I've changed so much in those years, but nobody notices, because it's all about him. And he never changes. All I want is to have a normally messed-up life, like other kids. I feel like I'm growing up in a hospital! And I'm too young to be a full-time nurse, even if it is for my dad. But see, it doesn't feel like he's my dad anymore. He's just like some guy who lives in our house and watches TV and rings a bell when he wants something. And we spend all our time looking after him. And my mom has just stopped being my mom, it's like I don't have any parents at all....

So I just had a small role in the school play, but when it came time for the show, I was the only one who didn't have any family there. Everyone else was so excited, running around backstage. Then they'd see me and try to say something nice, but it always came out sounding phony. And the teachers would come over and give me looks of pity, saying, "You poor girl" or "It's gonna get better, you'll see." Like I was the sick person! Me! Oh, boy, I really hated that. I mean, I love my dad. I really do. And I know we had lots of great times, like when we'd go for family picnics or on nature walks. My dad knew the names of all the plants, he knew which ones you could eat and which ones you shouldn't. But that was a long time ago! And I'm not a little kid anymore. I wish you'd just make up your mind, Dad! Either die or get better! 'Cause nothing in nature lives like this. And I can't do it anymore! (*A pause.*) But I will. As long as you need me. (SHE *closes her book, puts away her homework.*) What else can I do?

THE DIARY OF ANNE FRANK
(BASED ON THE BOOK ANNE FRANK: DIARY OF A YOUNG GIRL)

DRAMATIZED BY FRANCES GOODRICH AND ALBERT HACKETT

For two years during World War II, ANNE, *15, has lived with 6–and then 7–other Jews in "the Secret Annex," the cramped top floors of a Dutch spice warehouse and office building.* SHE *has become friends with, and received her first kiss from Peter, who is 3 years older—he is also living in confinement with the Franks and his family. Before the Nazis raid their hiding place—sending the inhabitants to concentration camps—*ANNE *consoles him.* SHE *talks to* PETER *about the uses of imagination—the walks* SHE *can take in the park, where* SHE *used to go with her father (nicknamed Pim), religion, and the true nature of people.*

SCENE

Peter's room, a loft over the stairwell, which has a skylight. Amsterdam, The Netherlands.

TIME

Friday, August 4, 1944.

ANNE: Look, Peter, the sky. (SHE *looks up through the skylight.*) What a lovely, lovely day! Aren't the clouds beautiful? You know what I do when it seems as if I couldn't stand being cooped up for one more minute? I *think* myself out. I think myself on a walk in the park where I used to go with Pim. Where the jonquils and the crocus and the violets grow down the slopes. You know the most wonderful part about *thinking* yourself out? You can have it any way you like. You can have roses and violets and chrysanthemums all blooming at the same time.... It's funny... I used to take it all for granted... and now I've gone crazy about everything to do with nature. Haven't you?

[Peter: I've just gone crazy. I think if something doesn't happen soon... if we don't get out of here... I can't stand much more of it!

Anne: (*Softly.*) I wish you had a religion, Peter.

[Peter: No, thanks! Not me!]

Anne: Oh, I don't mean you have to be Orthodox... or believe in heaven and hell and purgatory and things... I just mean some religion... it doesn't matter what. Just to believe in something! When I think of all that's out there... the trees... and flowers... and seagulls... when I think of the dearness of you, Peter... and the goodness of the people we know... Mr. Kraler, Miep, Dirk, the vegetable man, all risking their lives for us every day.... When I think of these good things, I'm not afraid any more... I find myself, and God, and I...

[(*Peter interrupts, getting up and walking away.*)

Peter: That's fine! But when I begin to think, I get mad! Look at us, hiding out for two years. Not able to move! Caught here like... waiting for them to come and get us... and all for what?]

Anne: We're not the only people that've had to suffer. There've always been people that've had to...sometimes one race...sometimes another...and yet...

[**Peter:** That doesn't make me feel any better!]

Anne: (*Going to him.*) I know it's terrible, trying to have any faith... when people are doing such horrible...but you know what I sometimes think? I think the world may be going through a phase, the way I was with Mother. It'll pass, maybe not for hundreds of years, but some day...I still believe, in spite of everything, that people are really good at heart.

[**Peter:** I want to see something now....Not a thousand years from now!

(*He goes over, sitting down again on the cot.*)]

Anne: But, Peter, if you'd only look at it as part of a great pattern... that we're just a little minute in the life...(She *breaks off.*) Listen to us, going at each other like a couple of stupid grownups! Look at the sky now. Isn't it lovely? (She *holds out her hand to him.* [*Peter takes it and rises, standing with her at the window looking out, his arms around her.*]) Some day, when we're outside again, I'm going to...(She *breaks off as* She *hears the sound of a car outside, its brakes squealing as it comes to a sudden stop.*)

DOG PEOPLE

BY KAYLA CAGAN

SAM *tries to convince her parents that it's time for the family to get a dog.*

SCENE
The living room of the family home.

TIME
Today.

SAM: (*To parents.*) Just hear me out. I know what you're going to say: "We're cat people." I know we already have two cats, but Bootsie and Collins don't belong to me. They belong to you guys. They sleep in your room, or the twins' room. The cats never sleep in my room, not that I care, but that isn't fair. You guys all come in sets. Mom and Dad. Andy and Candy. Bootsie and Collins. And then there's me. I look around and I don't see anybody else. There's nobody to do homework with or beat at hide and seek. Nobody climbs up on my bunk bed at night to tell ghost stories. Even the cats don't want to be by me, and it's not because I pull their tails. It's because they can tell. Mom and Dad, it's time you knew the truth, too. I've kept my secret too long. I'm not like you. I'm not a cat person. I'm a Dog Person. I like dogs and I'm always going to like dogs. Big ones, small ones, fast ones, old ones, shaggy ones, curly ones, smelly ones, and cuddly ones. Dogs like to play fetch with me. On my bike, they run next to me. When I whistle in the park, they jump and lick my face! No barks, no bites, just sloppy kisses and wagging tails. So, I hope you know what this means. We're going to have to get an awesome dog, and probably by this weekend. I'll let you have some time to discuss it among yourselves. I know it's a lot to process, but I hope you'll understand that cats and dogs can live together peacefully under one roof. I mean, look, I've managed to get along with you guys all these years. So dogs and cats—that should be a snap. (SAM *gives her parents a nod and walks off confidently towards the kitchen.*)

THE EFFECT OF GAMMA RAYS ON MAN-IN-THE-MOON MARIGOLDS

BY PAUL ZINDEL

TILLIE, *tweens to teens, lives with her disillusioned and abusive single mother and her sister who is mentally unstable and has a medical history of convulsions. Here,* TILLIE, *who is very shy, stands in front of her school science display.* SHE *is holding 3x5 cards and is very nervous as* SHE *refers to them, explaining her experiment. (This selection is a combination of two monologues from the play.)*

SCENE

At a school science fair in the New York City area. TILLIE*'s display consists of a three-panel screen and three pots of various mutations of marigolds.*

TIME

In the '60s or whenever someone contemplates the wonders of the universe.

TILLIE: *The Past*: The seeds were exposed to various degrees of gamma rays from radiation sources in Oak Ridge. (*Pause.*) Mr. Goodman helped me pay for the seeds. (*Pause.*) Their growth was plotted against…time. (*The first gong rings.* SHE *crosses to the left of the display.*) *The Present*: The seeds which received little radiation have grown to plants which are normal in appearance. The seeds which received moderate radiation gave rise to mutations such as double blooms, giant stems, and variegated leaves. The seeds closest to the gamma source were killed or yielded dwarf plants. (*Gong.*) *The Future*: After radiation is better understood a day will come when the power from exploding atoms will change the whole world we know. (*With inspiration.*) Some of the mutations will be good ones—wonderful things beyond our dreams—and I believe, I believe this with all my heart, THE DAY WILL COME WHEN MANKIND WILL THANK GOD FOR THE STRANGE AND BEAUTIFUL ENERGY FROM THE ATOM. (*Distant applause is heard. The lights fade to a single soft light on* TILLIE*'s face. Distant electronic sounds are heard. With a soft cry.*) Mama! (*Again with a soft cry.*) Mama!...

THE CONCLUSION: My experiment has shown some of the strange effects radiation can produce...and how dangerous it can be if not handled correctly. Mr. Goodman said I should tell in this conclusion what my future plans are and how this experiment has helped me make them. For one thing, the Effect of Gamma Rays on Man-in-the-Moon Marigolds has made me curious about the sun and the stars, for the universe itself must be like a world of great atoms—and I want to know more about it. (*The room is dark now except for a light on* TILLIE.) But most important, I suppose...(SHE *moves to the railing right of the stairs, and faces right.*) my experience has made me feel important—every atom in me, in everybody, has come from the sun—(SHE *slowly faces front.*) from places beyond our dreams. The atoms of our hands, the atoms of our hearts...Atom. Atom. What a beautiful word.

EYES WIDE OPEN

BY JENNIFER KIRKEBY

KRISTIN, *a 14-year-old dancer, tells her best friend about a weird dream that* SHE *had.*

SCENE

Dance studio.

TIME

The next day.

KRISTIN: Oh, I had this really weird dream last night. Do you want to hear it? I was on this high dive.…Oh, you know that I'm afraid of heights, right? Yeah, really terrified. So I'm up on this high dive, and I'm scared to death. All these kids are lined up on the ladder behind me, yelling, "Jump! Hurry up! We're getting cold!" I'm stepping closer and closer to the edge of the board. I finally get there, and I freeze. I can't move. I'm supposed to dive to pass some swimming test, but I can't. I can't even jump. My knees are shaking, and I feel like I'm going to die. Finally, the coach comes up to me and says, "Can you do this?" I tell her, "No. I can't." So, she takes my hand and very carefully leads me to the back of the board. She tells all of the kids to go back down the ladder. I'm embarrassed and humiliated, but it's okay because at least now I know that I'm safe. Oh, but here's the really weird part. The coach was my grandma, who died five years ago. It made me realize how much I miss her. You know? I could talk to her about anything. I've never been that close to anyone else. Maybe I never will be. (*Pause.*) So what about you? Did you have any weird dreams? Come on, tell me. I told you mine.

FORMALDEHYDE

BY ANDY BRAGEN

CHARLENE *examines a set of petri dishes.* SHE*'s a precocious 12-year-old whose light blue dress is too tight—*SHE*'s chubby. Her science experiment, which captivates her, regards formaldehyde, the growth of bacteria, and the decay of dead tissue.*

SCENE

At home in small-town Mississippi.

TIME

1950s.

CHARLENE: I am an amoeba. My arms, my legs, my face, they've gooped together, mutating into one big oozy blob. I slosh when I walk. I have no eyes, no lips, no feet, no butt—I consist entirely of yellow slime. I am incredibly tiny, tinier than the tiniest ant. I live in a petri dish.

(SHE *examines her dishes.*)

I am nourished by the darkness. It helps me grow and grow until I reach the moment of bisection.

(SHE *contorts.*)

The moment has arrived. I feel my destiny calling. I follow the history of generations of amoebae, the call of my species. I will divide.

(SHE *contorts herself, pretending to divide.*)

Oof! Oww! OOO! Ahhhh! I am alone no more.

(*Talking to the other amoebae.*)

Hi, there, what's your name...Charlene? My name is Charlene, too. Isn't that a coincidence? Are we going to be friends?...We are, aren't we? We're going to be friends!

(*Shaking her own hand.*)

Hello! Hello! It's a pleasure to make your acquaintance.

GEEK

BY CRYSTAL SKILLMAN

HONEY, *mid-teens, and her friend Danya are racing through a role-playing convention. They want to meet the Japanese anime artist Samagashi, for whom they, along with* HONEY*'s recently deceased sister, Ellen—a suicide—have created a comic book. As it's a "cos-playing" event, everyone in the con is dressed like their favorite Samagashi character (*HONEY *is dressed like Virgie, the trusty "right-hand gal" and guide to the lead in* DANTE'S FIRE, *a huge manga). But here,* SHE'S *lost her way—*SHE'S *had a fight with Danya and teamed up with another cos-player dressed like a big fuzzy ball-like creature—named Squeaker. They were trying to get back their comic, which was stolen—and now it's found. High off the chase,* HONEY *confides in Squeaker (spoiler alert: who turns out to be the guy* SHE *likes at school, but* SHE *has no idea because he's dressed up!).*

SCENE

At an anime role-playing convention named Dante's Fire Con in Columbus, Ohio—5 hours away from home.

TIME

The last half hour of Dante's Fire Con. It's about to close!

HONEY: We got my bag back—yes! (*The lost comic is in the bag.*) Oh man you are the best! I'm Honey. I mean in real life. When

I'm not dressed like—Virgie! That's me! A trusty right-hand gal and guide who always knows everything and where she's going and is so confident and cool!! Just like me, right? Right. But, seriously, thanks. What's in here is very important to me, so thanks and, uh…I love your outfit—Squeaker is so yellow and big and cute. He's my favorite character and you look great, and I never met anyone who loved Squeaker more than me! Well, thanks again. I bet you have to go. I mean this place closes in like thirty minutes—I can't imagine you want to spend your last few minutes with a stranger.

[(*He squeaks, starts to go.*)]

Most people think your character, Squeaker, was put in the *Dante's Fire* TV show to use as exposition so my character Virgie could spill her guts when everything went wrong.

And man, why is everything going so wrong?

We got what we wanted. But I don't know what to do. I know this isn't your problem but—you aren't going to take your costume off, are you.

[(*He shakes his head no, like a kid.*)]

You're going to keep playing—

[(*He shakes his head yes.*)]

Because you obviously spent a lot of time on that costume and look at those ears! You've even got some spy-looking, super faraway hearing device in there—because that's Squeaker's skill.

[(*He is excited* SHE *notices this, nuzzles her.*)]

OK.

Squeaker?

I've been pretty mad lately.

And now I've got what we made—what my sister and Danya and I—we've been working on for so long. What we wanted to show Samagashi until…

It's really messed up, and I don't have anyone to talk to…!

Well, there's Danya and, sure, we're supposed to be like best friends, but we're not talking right now, OK?!

[(*Squeaker tries to squeak something nice.*)]

Yeah, I guess you're a good friend, too, but it's not the same. I just met you like ten seconds ago and you could be some totally weirdo crazy guy in some fuzzball cos-playing outfit.

[(*Squeaker is sad and kinda offended.*)]

I didn't mean—whoever you are! Squeaker.

[(*Squeaker jumps up and down.*)]

I like being your friend, I like having adventures, I like having someone to listen to me but that's not all I need. Because I don't believe it. I don't believe it, but I'm going to say it.

A few days ago my sister died.

And Danya and I we don't talk about it—we just—we come here. We come here like it's some kind of quest, like if we meet Samagashi, who created all these characters we loved and show her what we created because we loved—like that would change anything? Because I miss my sister I love my sister but she's not—she's not coming back.

Danya, she acts like she doesn't need anyone. But she does. She needs me, even if she's not good with words. Saying them. She's great at writing them.

And sometimes people may say things, but they can't say them the exact way you need to hear them. I mean this—real life–you and me here—this isn't a show—sometimes things just come out wrong, and you can't change it. And sometimes people do things that are wrong, and they can't change it. But if you realize all this—you can do something. I can!

I have to find Danya. Because she's just as hurt as I am. And if I help her, I can hurt less because—it's not her fault. She is who she is. And I am who I am. And Honey isn't anything like Virgie, but that's why I like playing her—because it's making me the Honey I want to be!

Because the Honey I am right now is just laughed at for liking the coolest kid in school.

[(*Squeaker nods.*)]

Like that's going to work out—being in love with Bobby Branden.

[(*Squeaker makes surprised noise.*)]

I know there's no way *the* cutest guy in school would ever be into me but—

[(*Squeaker kisses her.*)]

Well, I know you love me, Squeaker, I raised you from an egg on the planet of Glock! And I am changing. I am growing up or something, I think. I'm sure whoever you are—you are really my friend, too? And so is Danya. And she needs me. I have to find her. And I'll be totally cool alone—don't worry—don't worry about me at all, no siree—

[(*Squeaker licks her with a big orange tongue.*)]

Aw! You hugged me! Because we're friends, too! Right! I'm so glad you want to go with me. But where do we go? Where can we find Danya? Samagashi! Right—I bet she's already there! We'll go to Samagashi together! Danya'll be there. And everything will be OK! We'll be OK!

GOING HOME

BY SUSAN ROWAN MASTERS

ANNIE, *12-14, is mourning the loss of her grandma, who raised her. Her mom has never been there for her, and* ANNIE *doesn't want anything to do with her when she shows up. Then something happens on the way to the funeral.*

SCENE

A trailer park in southern Pennsylvania.

TIME

In the present, talking about the past.

ANNIE: (*Sits, writing a letter to her mother.*) Maybe it was destiny that our car hit that pothole on the way to Gram's funeral. I like to think so anyway. I mean, it gave us all a jolt at the time, and for a moment I was afraid that we were gonna go off the road. But if that hadn't happened, then things between me and Ma might never have changed. I really believe that. (SHE *writes the letter, stops.*) Because, you see, my Gram was more mom to me than my Ma ever was. Ma just showed up two weeks ago to help out before Gram died. I think it was guilt for all the years she wasn't around. Ma had me at eighteen and then dumped me off with her folks. Well, there wasn't anyone who could have brought me up better than Gram and Pop...and I still saw Ma twice a year, when she drove down from Pittsburgh in her beat-up Plymouth. "Soon as I get a better job and a decent place I'm taking you with me," she'd say. But Ma always went back alone....(SHE *finishes writing her letter, looks up.*) The morning of Gram's funeral, Ma had come into the bathroom and found me bawling my eyes out. "Oh honey," she said, reaching for me. I just shook my head. I wasn't ready to have anyone paw me, especially Ma. But when the funeral car hit that pothole, I saw Ma looking at us, Pop and me. I noticed her red puffy eyes. I realized she was hurting, too. I reached over and took Ma's hand into mine. For the rest of the ride home we sat there, Ma and Pop and me, holding on to each other. I believe that things are going to be different now. I really do. (SHE *folds up the letter, puts it in the envelope, smiles.*)

HAMLET

BY WILLIAM SHAKESPEARE

OPHELIA, *about 15, is the daughter of Polonius, Lord Chamberlain of the Danish court.* SHE *has been forbidden to see Prince Hamlet because, as royalty, he cannot marry her. Here,* OPHELIA *tells her father that Hamlet has met her, nevertheless, and acted as if he was crazy. This prompts Polonius to believe that the prince is in love with his daughter. Actually, Hamlet is pretending to be mad so he can avenge his father's murder.*

SCENE

In Denmark: Elsinore castle; in the quarters of Polonius.

TIME

The late middle ages, spring...or let your imagination go.

OPHELIA: My lord, as I was sewing in my closet,
Lord Hamlet, with his doublet all unbrac'd,
No hat upon his head, his stockings foul'd,
Ungart'red, and down-gyved to his ankle;
Pale as his shirt, his knees knocking each other,
And with a look so piteous in purport
As if he had been loosed out of hell
To speak of horrors—he comes before me.

[Polonius: Mad for thy love?]

Ophelia: My lord, I do not know,
But truly I do fear it.

[Polonius: What said he?]

Ophelia: He took me by the wrist and held me hard;
Then goes he to the length of all his arm,
And, with his other hand thus o'er his brow,
He falls to such perusal of my face
As he would draw it. Long stay'd he so.
At last, a little shaking of mine arm,
And thrice his head thus waving up and down,
He rais'd a sigh so piteous and profound
As it did seem to shatter all his bulk
And end his being. That done, he lets me go,
And with his head over his shoulder turn'd
He seem'd to find his way without his eyes,
For out a'doors he went without their help
And to the last bended their light on me.

HAMLET

BY WILLIAM SHAKESPEARE

OPHELIA, *about 15, has gone insane after the death of her father, Polonius (Hamlet killed him, thinking he was the king). Singing of her sorrow with her hair down,* SHE *offers flowers and herbs.*

SCENE

Elsinore, a castle in Denmark.

TIME

The late Middle Ages, spring, or you might have a better conceptualization.

OPHELIA: (*Sings.*)

They bore him barefac'd on the bier
(Hey non nony, nony, hey nony)
And in his grave rain'd many a tear.
Fare you well, my dove!

[LAERTES: Hadst thou thy wits, and didst persuade revenge,
It could not move thus.]

OPHELIA: You must sing "A-down a-down, and you call him a-down-a."
O, how the wheel becomes it! It is the false steward, that stole his master's daughter.

[LAERTES: This nothing's more than matter.]

OPHELIA: There's rosemary, that's for remembrance. Pray you, love, remember. And there is pansies, that's for thoughts.

[LAERTES: A document in madness! Thoughts and remembrance fitted.]

OPHELIA: There's fennel for you, and columbines. There's rue for you, and here's some for me. We may call it herb of grace o' Sundays. O, you must wear your rue with a difference! There's a daisy. I would give you some violets, but they wither'd all when my father died. They say he made a good end.

(*Sings.*) For bonny sweet Robin is all my joy.

[LAERTES: Thought and affliction, passion, hell itself,
She turns to favour and to prettiness.]

OPHELIA: (*Sings.*)
And will he not come again?
And will he not come again?
No, no, he is dead;
Go to thy deathbed;
He never will come again.
His beard was as white as snow,
All flaxen was his poll.
He is gone, he is gone,
And we cast away moan.
God ha' mercy on his soul!
And of all Christian souls, I pray God. God b' wi' you.

(SHE *exits.*)

HOLLYWOOD ARMS

BY CARRIE HAMILTON AND CAROL BURNETT

Arriving home from school, HELEN, *9, hears her estranged father, Jody, knocking at the door. He weaves unsteadily on his feet, drunk.*

SCENE

A one-room apartment, one block north of Hollywood Boulevard in Hollywood, California.

TIME

1941.

HELEN: Daddy…?

[JODY: Just one li'l beer, Punk. That's all I had. She's gone to heaven… your Grandma Nora's gone…in the ground. (HELEN *looks very worried. Choosing his words carefully.*) Just needed to steady my nerves, y'know? I miss her.]

HELEN: [I miss her, too, Daddy.] (*Beat.*) Why don't you come in and sit down? You just need to sit down. [(SHE *helps him over to the couch. He teeters on the edge.*)] *You* rest for a minute, I'll whip up some coffee for you. (HELEN *goes into the kitchen and frantically looks for coffee and a clean cup in the messy kitchen. Calling from the kitchen.*) That's all you need. A good cup of coffee! (HELEN *has found the percolator, turned on the tap to fill the coffee pot. As*

SHE'*s frantically throwing the coffee into the pot and putting it on the stove,* [*Jody slowly slides off the couch, winding up on the floor*]. HELEN *calls to him from the kitchen.*) Hey, Daddy! I got the part in the play at school! Isn't that wonderful? I'm nervous to do it in front of an audience, but Mrs. McNeil says that even the most seasoned professional…(HELEN *turns around and sees Jody passed out cold.*) Daddy? [(HELEN, *alarmed, bends down and touches her father.*)] Daddy? Are you all right? [(*Jody moans, and* HELEN *begins to shake him.*)] Wake up. Please, Daddy, please be all right. Wake up! (SHE *starts to cry* [*and shakes him harder*].) Don't do this! Wake up! Please! Don't do this! Daddy!

[JODY: (*Almost inaudible, waving her off.*) Go 'way…]

HELEN: Look at me! Look at me! Wake up! Don't do this! (HELEN, *hysterical, screams in his face.* [*He mumbles something again, tries to sit up and falls back down.*])

[JODY:…do…well…]

HELEN: I prayed for you, just like you said! Wake up! I prayed for you! I prayed for you! Wake up! (HELEN *is screaming down at him at the top of her lungs, crying her heart out.* [*Dixie and Malcolm run in.*])

[DIXIE: Helen! What is it? What's wrong with you?

MALCOLM: What's she screamin' about?]

HELEN: I hate you! I hate you! [(*Malcolm sees Jody.*)

MALCOLM: Oh, brother! Get a gander of this. (*Dixie spots Jody, bends down and smells his breath.*] HELEN *is still crying.*)

[DIXIE: Out like a light. C'mon Jody, let's get you up. (*Dixie tries to lift Jody.*) Malcolm, for godsakes, help me out here! (*They're unsuccessful.*] HELEN *runs to the pull-down bed and curls up in it, crying into a pillow.*)

THE ILIAD

BY CRAIG WRIGHT

In Craig Wright's dramatization of Homer, girls—in the original production the tiniest girls played the meanest parts—portray heroes and gods. Boys can, of course, play these roles, too. In this monologue, ACHILLES, *bold warrior of the Trojan War—and quick to anger—confronts Agamemnon, general of the Greek army.*

SCENE

A ravaged, war-torn, no man's land: dangerous-looking and destroyed.

TIME

Mythic time.

ACHILLES: I'd sooner take to my ships and go home than stay here
One more day and be disgraced by you while you pile up
Prizes you never earned!...(You) will take Briseis [a loved slave] from (me) just to show (me)—Just to show me what?
How powerful you are? How mighty?
Coward! Never *once* have you armed yourself and gone into battle with the rest of us! No, you'd rather stride around the camp giving orders, watching us die, and then taking our prizes if, by the grace of the gods, we live! I'll have no part in it! None!
But this I swear: soon, Agamemnon, very soon, you will be in need of me.

Desperate need. And when your men are being cut down
by the hand of Hector, you will bitterly regret this day!

THE ILIAD

BY CRAIG WRIGHT

PRIAM is very old, the last king of Troy. His eldest son—Hector, the great warrior—has been killed by Achilles—the leader of the Greeks. Here, PRIAM asks for his son's body.

SCENE

The remnants of broken buildings, shattered by explosions, form the basic structure of this place: concrete; rusted metal; trashcans; tires; an overturned blue rolling chair; a mannequin; and a few dolls on the ground.

TIME

Among the ancients, today, tomorrow—or any time in between.

(PRIAM *kneels before Achilles.*)

PRIAM: I know what you're thinking, Achilles.

[ACHILLES: What am I thinking?]

PRIAM: You're thinking my son Hector was proud:
that he deserved to die, if not for his faults,
then at least in recompense for the Achaeans he's killed.
Or, perhaps, you think he deserved to die merely
because he chose the life of a soldier.

Thoughts like that have occurred to me, not just about Hector,
but about myself: about all of us assembled here.
But hear me out. Like you, Achilles, like all of us,
Hector was more than a soldier:
to me, he was also a son, and a child, and no matter how tall
he grew or how fierce, I never stopped seeing, behind his
resolute eyes,
the sweet uncertainty of the boy (*After a beat.*)
Achilles, we men have bloodied this shore long enough.
If it be the will of the gods to extend this war, so be it:
but for now, please, I beg you, grant me my son's body.
Grant me that peace.

INCONSOLABLE

BY ISRAEL HOROVITZ

A Daughter, *11-13, remembers the worst day of her life.*

SCENE

The family home.

TIME

The present.

Daughter: I found her in the garage. She was inside the car and there was this hose taped to the exhaust pipe and then taped in through the window. She had taped this note to the car window asking me to forgive her, telling me it wasn't about me, it was about her—telling me to leave her in the car and to call my father and that it wasn't my fault.

(*A beat.*) I tried to get the car door open, but it was locked from the inside. I pulled the hose out of the window, and I broke the window open with one of my father's golf clubs and I shut off the engine by turning the key. I opened the garage door and dragged her onto the driveway into fresh air, figuring that could help, but she was definitely dead by then. The doctors all said that she was definitely dead. I called 911, and then I called my father. (*A beat.*) It's only been a couple'a weeks, since it happened, so, I'm still pretty numb. I'll be okay.

"IN THE LAND OF MY BIRTH" FROM NO WORD IN GUYANESE FOR ME

BY WENDY GRAF

Teenage HANNA, *14, remembers her childhood in Guyana and the death of her mother.*

SCENE

In HANNA*'s imagination, reliving her past.*

TIME

Before.

HANNA: In the land of my birth I run through the tall grasses.... My toes go squish, squish, squishing through the clay...the rich, red Guyanese dirt...*pit a pat, pit a pat...*frogs leap out of the way.... "Here I come! Here...comes...Hanna!" I brush da mosquitos from my face away as I run over da wet earth, skipping over da rocks, da pebbles, around holes and black bushes, under da ferns, up and down da summer path. And da wings of da flies glisten silver and blue and beautiful like da fairy wings in da sun as they circle da fruit, circle da plums, da oranges, da pears, da sticky tings dat drop from da trees...I can smell da sweet of da fruit as I run, run, run. Swallows swoop and fly....Is dat a hummingbird? Is it? Den hop hop hop over da rotted nuts and berries and da vegetable thingy that me na like...."You can't catch me, you can't catch *me, Buddy, Buddy*!" My big brothers, dey laugh. "We give you head start, Hanna Banana!" We collapse, laughing, breathing, panting so very hard at da edge of da stream, den dip our brown feet with da red mud into da cool, cool still watah.... Ahhhhhh...da mud swims away and wiggle de toes like little crabs, den kick, kick, kick, kick, kick! Buddy say, "Hanna, you make *hassa lookanannie* run away with your splashes!" And we are happy, so happy dat day in our Guyana, in our land of so many watahs....That was before. Before Mumma died in the fire. Before "God rest da dead in da living and da looking," before Nine Night, before "No sweeping da house. Cover da mirrors." (*Plaintive cry.*) Mumma! (*No answer.*)

IPHIGENIA IN AULIS
BY EURIPIDES

Agamemnon, the commander-in-chief of the Greek army, sends for his daughter IPHIGENIA, *14.* SHE *believes* SHE *will be married to Achilles, a future hero of the Trojan War. Instead,* IPHIGENIA *discovers that* SHE *is to be killed to appease the goddess Artemis.*

SCENE
The ancient Greek coast where ships wait to sail.

TIME
1194 B.C.

IPHIGENIA: O my father—
If I had the tongue of Orpheus
So that I could charm with song the stones to
Leap and follow me, or if my words could
Quite beguile anyone I wished—I'd use
My magic now. But only with tears can I
Make arguments and here I offer them.
O father,
My body is a suppliant's, tight clinging
To your knees. Do not take away this life
Of mine before its dying time. Nor make me
Go down under the earth to see the world
Of darkness, for it is sweet to look on

The day's light.
I was first to call you father,
You to call me child. And of your children
First to sit upon your knees. We kissed
Each other in our love. "O child,"
You said, "surely one day I shall see you
Happy in your husband's home. And like
A flower blooming for me and in my honor."
Then as I clung to you and wove my fingers
In your beard, I answered, "Father, you,
Old and reverent then, with love I shall
Receive into my home, and so repay you
For the years of trouble and your fostering
Care of me." I have in memory all these words
Of yours and mine. But you, forgetting,

Have willed it in your heart to kill me.
Oh no—by Pelops
And by Atreus, your father, and
By my mother who suffered travail
At my birth and now must suffer a second
Time for me! Oh, oh—the marriage
Of Paris and Helen—Why must it touch
My life? Why must Paris be my ruin?
Father, look at me, and into my eyes;
Kiss me, so that if my words fail,
And if I die, this thing of love I may
Hold in my heart and remember.

(*Turning to Orestes, her young brother.*)

My brother, so little can you help us
Who love you, but weep with me and
Beg your father not to kill your sister.

Oh, the threat of evil is instinct,
Even in a child's heart. See, even
Without speech, he begs you, Father,
Pity and have mercy on my sister's life.
Yes, both of us beseech you, this little child
And I, your daughter grown. So these words
Are all my argument. Let me win life
From you. I must. To look upon the world
Of light is for all men their greatest joy—
The shadow world below is nothing.
Men are mad, I say, who pray for death;
It is better that we live ever so
Miserably than die in glory.

LEMONADE

BY JERI WEISS

NATALIE, *age 10-11, wants to be the top seller in her school's fundraiser, but how can* SHE *win the grand prize when her own father won't even help?*

SCENE

A suburban neighborhood.

TIME

Right now.

NATALIE: (SHE *holds a lemon, tossing it from hand to hand at intervals.*) We were having this fundraiser at school, and if I sold a hundred rolls of wrapping paper by a certain weekend, I would win this big stuffed bear! That's what I told my mother when I got home from school. I hoped that she would buy some, but she said that I had to speak with my father. I didn't expect him to be very supportive, and that's what I got. (*Imitating her father.*) "You know what gripes me?" he said. "They take these kids out of class, tempt them with some lousy prizes, and then expect us to peddle their overpriced wrapping paper." I couldn't believe he wouldn't buy any. Not one roll. I even told him how Mrs. Brooks said it would help build our resourcefulness, but he wasn't budging. Then I made the mistake of uttering the three words certain to make even the most patient parent go ballistic: "That's not fair." Yep, I should have kept that one to myself. You can imagine how well that went over: (*Imitating her father.*) "I'm gonna tell you something my old man told me, so listen up. Do you know what you do when life hands you lemons? You make lemonade." Lemonade? I didn't want lemonade. I wanted the big stuffed bear. Then, when I asked him to take me out to sell on Saturday, he said he couldn't because he had to work, he wouldn't be around. And even when my mother asked him nicely, he still refused. (*Imitating her father.*) "You two don't appreciate how hard I work to put food on the table. I have an important project at the office, and I don't want to hear another word about it." (*A beat.*)

Well, it was obvious he wasn't going to help me at all, so I decided to go out on my own. But at every door, I got the same answer: (*Imitating different voices.*) "Sorry, honey, I just bought some from the kid down the street." Or "My son's selling it at his school, too." Or "I just gave all my money to the Girl Scouts." Girl Scouts. Don't get me started. With their Thin Mints and their Do-Si-Dos. How am I supposed to compete with that? I mean, my wrapping paper's nice and all, but it's not dipped in creamy milk chocolate. (*A beat.*)

I was about to go home, but there was one more house on the block. I thought about the big stuffed bear, and it was almost as if he were encouraging me to give it one last try. I rang the doorbell: no answer. "Darn!" But as I was leaving, a golf cart pulled into the driveway. The driver was surprised to see me come around the corner. But he wasn't nearly as surprised as the man sitting next to him in his checkered golf shorts and his lucky sun visor. It was my father. (*A beat.*) I guess Mrs. Brooks was right about building our resourcefulness. Because even though my father told a big whopping lie to me and my mother about having to work,

I didn't get upset, and I didn't get angry, and I didn't get sad. I just got the bear. And you know what I named him? Lemonade. Because that's what you get when life hands you lemons. Right, Dad?

MARICELA DE LA LUZ LIGHTS THE WORLD

BY JOSÉ RIVERA

Faced with many unreal events on a surreal journey through Los Angeles, MARICELA, *around 11, is forced to declare what* SHE *believes in.*

SCENE
Los Angeles.

TIME
Now.

MARICELA: I believe in food. I believe in words. I believe in arithmetic. I believe in gravity. I believe you only live once. I believe you only get one chance to do all this and after you die that's it. IT. I think your job while you're alive is to know as much as possible of reality and life and, sure, you're never going to know everything. There will always be mysteries. But I think the more you know...the more you will pass on to your children... until, someday, we will know everything, all the secrets, all the mysteries, and then, maybe, we'll finally be happy. (*A beat.*) I'm facing sixth grade next year—assuming I ever get home! I'm half Puerto Rican and half Swedish. I'm facing a city where people want to know on what side of the race line you fall. Half Latino, half Anglo; half East Coast, half West Coast; half child, half teen—divorced parents—oh, check it out!—we moved all the way to Los Angeles just so Mami can be with her boyfriend, this guy Jason who wants to be a star but can't even ACT—and you wonder why I don't believe in anything magical?

MARICELA DE LA LUZ LIGHTS THE WORLD

BY JOSÉ RIVERA

OFELIA, *12-14, one of the characters we meet on a mythic journey through Los Angeles, explains how* SHE *became the goddess of the Los Angeles River.*

SCENE
Los Angeles.

TIME
Now.

OFELIA: Now, I wasn't always a goddess. I came to the West Coast long ago to be an actress. I knew Greta Garbo. She was a friend of mine. I lent her money, you know. I gave her advice on how to speak and what clothes to wear and who to be seen with. Oh, we cut quite a figure, the two of us! Going to parties! Openings! We were gods back then! But...you know...it's a fickle business. Greta took off like a meteor. But I'm Latina and there wasn't any work for a Latina actress. Even Greta rejected me. So I quit the business and decided to take up meditation and I sat and I meditated and I sat and I meditated—until!—I was transformed utterly! I became a goddess and started protecting the L.A. River as it flowed lazily through the city. Once upon a time people could wash their clothes in my waters! Children could swim in me! I sustained frogs and herons and quenched the thirsts of coyotes and Gila monsters. But I kept shifting my banks, upsetting the money men and developers who had their way and poured concrete all over me and straightened me up and made me into nothing but a glorified drainage ditch! Look at my hair! Just filled with Coke cans! Very upsetting! But I persevere! I follow and protect my darling river as any good river goddess should—as if it were the Nile itself!

THE MEMBER OF THE WEDDING

BY CARSON MCCULLERS

FRANKIE ADDAMS *is 12 and five-sixths years old: tall, awkward, dreamy, and restless,* SHE *has a boy's haircut. Her brother, who is in the army, is getting married in two days and* FRANKIE *would like to go on the honeymoon with the newlyweds. Wanting to "become connected or identified with a world larger than that which confines her," according to the play's first director, Harold Clurman,* FRANKIE *doesn't have any friends.* SHE *spends most of her time in and around the kitchen of her house with John Henry, her 6-year-old cousin, and Berenice, the maid.*

SCENE

Outside the kitchen, in the yard of the Addams' house in a small Southern town. Here, an elm tree grows and a sheet, used as a stage curtain, hangs at the side of an arbor.

TIME

Early evening in August, 1945.

FRANKIE: Don't bother me, John Henry. I'm thinking.

[JOHN HENRY: What you thinking about?]

Frankie: About the wedding. About my brother and the bride. Everything's been so sudden today. I never believed before about the fact that the earth turns at the rate of about a thousand miles a day. I didn't understand why it was that if you jumped up in the air you wouldn't land in Selma or Fairview or somewhere else instead of the same back yard. But now it seems to me I feel the world going around very fast. (Frankie *begins turning around in circles with arms outstretched. John Henry copies her. They both turn.*) I feel it turning and it makes me dizzy.

[**John Henry:** I'll stay and spend the night with you.]

Frankie: (*Suddenly stopping her turning.*) [No.] I just now thought of something.

[**John Henry:** You just a little while ago was begging me.]

Frankie: I know where I'm going.

[(*There are sounds of children playing in the distance.*)

John Henry: Let's go play with the children, Frankie.]

Frankie: I tell you I know where I'm going. It's like I've known it all my life. Tomorrow I will tell everybody.

[**John Henry:** Where?]

Frankie: (*Dreamily.*) After the wedding I'm going with them to Winter Hill. I'm going off with them after the wedding.

[**John Henry:** You serious?]

FRANKIE: [Shush,] just now I realized something. The trouble with me is that for a long time I have been just an "I" person. All other people can say "we." When Berenice says "we" she means her lodge and church and colored people. Soldiers can say "we" and mean the army. All people belong to a "we" except me.

[JOHN HENRY: What are we going to do?]

FRANKIE: Not to belong to a "we" makes you too lonesome. Until this afternoon I didn't have a "we," but now after seeing Janice and Jarvis I suddenly realize something.

[JOHN HENRY: What?]

FRANKIE: I know that the bride and my brother are the "we" of me. So I'm going with them, and joining with the wedding. This coming Sunday when my brother and the bride leave this town, I'm going with the two of them to Winter Hill. And after that to whatever place that they will ever go. (*There is a pause.*) I love the two of them so much and we belong to be together. I love the two of them so much because they are the *we* of me.

MINI'S YARD SALE

BY ASHER WYNDHAM

MINI, *a young Mexican-American girl, is coloring in some letters on a piece of paper with magic markers.* SHE *is talking to a classmate about her family's recent yard sale.*

SCENE

An art classroom.

TIME

The present, during school hours.

MINI: The sign looked like this— (SHE *shows a piece of paper that reads "YARD SALE! CHEAP! CHEAP!"*) I taped the sign to a box and put rocks in the box. The sign had to be nice 'cause my mom wanted it to be busy-busy like half-price day at Salvation Army. My mom said to me, like a week before the yard sale, "Mini, some of our things need to go on the sale table." Why? I asked her. "We need more money to go," my mom told me. Go where? I asked. "California," she said. I wasn't a little girl anymore, but I cried like one. "Pack our things—not everything—only necessary things," my mom said. So no spatulas, coffee maker, Bratz dolls, my dad's coats and hats, blender, and lampshades. All of it was cheap cheap. We needed it all to sell 'cause we needed money so we could buy gas for Maria's van. We needed money so we could leave Phoenix before my mom got sent back in a bus to… where she came from. When people started parking nearby and coming to the yard sale, I was thinking…we are not bad people. We dream just like you. We just want a home ….Have I found a new home here? I like it here in California…I like my new art class. I am going to draw my new apartment and you're going to be in it, 'cause you're my new friend. (MINI *turns the paper over and starts coloring.*)

MY CHOICE

BY CHLOE WHITEHORN

LISA, *a 14-year-old girl who prides herself on making decisions about everything concerned with her life, finds that this becomes a problem when* SHE *tries to control the circumstances leading to her first kiss.*

SCENE
School hallway.

TIME
This moment.

LISA: I'm not a victim. In the fourteen years I've been alive, everything in my life has been my choice. Things don't just happen to me, I make them happen. I choose. My dad says that I even chose when I was born. Mom's labor started when he was out of town so I stayed inside until he finished his meeting and drove back from Ottawa and was in the hospital room with my mom, so I could have my whole family there. 'Cause it was my day. I don't do anything that I don't want to. It's my life and I'm going to live it the way I want to. I make the choices....So the first time I kissed a boy it wasn't gonna be some random guy during some dumb spin-the-bottle game at a party in someone's musky basement rec room. It was going to be a major first so I wanted it to be perfect, you know what I mean?

I chose Brandon. He's cute enough that I wouldn't be embarrassed to say I kissed him, but not so cute that people'd be like, "Yeah, so? He kisses everyone." We'd been flirting all year, so when I asked him if he wanted to hang out after school, it wasn't like, out of nowhere. He said he had an hour to kill before hockey practice and I should come to his place 'cause his parents wouldn't be home. (*A beat.*) Walking to his house, I carried my backpack on my left shoulder even though it kept slipping off, just so my right hand was free in case he wanted to, you know, hold it. But he didn't.

His house was warm. My house is always cold when I get home because the thermostat is set low when nobody's home, but his place was warm. Warm and decorated, like a museum. Didn't wanna touch anythin' so I just sat. I sat down in the middle of the couch though, so he would have to sit close to me. It wasn't like in the movies. He didn't look deep into my eyes and whisper compliments. Everything was really fast. His hands were rough. He didn't brush my hair away from my face like they do in the movies. I tasted gum, and um, my shampoo. I think, my bra, it got pulled down. He didn't even look at me. And he…I don't know. I thought we were just gonna kiss. (*A beat.*)

I know what everybody's been saying, and seriously, I'd rather they think that stuff about me than think I didn't want it. That I was some sort of victim, you know. I'm not going to say that he "took advantage" or whatever. I mean, yeah, I thought we were just gonna make out but….Even if I didn't want to do… what we did…we did it, so…so this isn't something that just happened to me. Right? I mean, it's my life, so I get to choose how I remember this…and if I tell anybody. And I choose not to. Why does anybody else have to know?

MY LIFE SO FAR

BY EDITH ANN, AS TOLD TO JANE WAGNER

EDITH ANN *is 6 years old and has written a book about her life so far—her thoughts about what* SHE *has learned, what* SHE *thinks of adults, and what* SHE*'s looking forward to as* SHE *grows up.*

SCENE
In a rocking chair at her home.

TIME
The present.

EDITH ANN: Hey! My name is Edith Ann, and I am six years old. The *hardest* part about being a kid is knowing you have got your whole life ahead of you. We have to learn everything from scratch: how to walk, how to talk, how to dress, how to go potty, how to tell time. But, as soon as I learned to tell time, I began arriving late everywhere.

Six is a big turning point; you do not want to make any mistakes. That is why you see a lot of six-year-olds behaving like they're still five. Here's something adults say that I do not like, "Edith Ann, what do you want to be when you grow up?" As if what I am now is not good enough. And my parents always tell me, "Edith Ann, just be yourself." Then, when I am being myself, they say, "Stop doing that!" They never seem to get that I was just being myself. Either they do not know who I really am or I'm not really what they had in mind. They did everything to get me to walk and talk, and now they just want me to sit down and shut up! I wish I had a quarter for every time my parents tell me I'm being childish. Shouldn't a kid my age have the right to *be* childish? It's one of the few perks we have left! Anyway, I wish my parents would act more like grown-ups. But, it just does not seem to work. Acting childish seems to come naturally, but acting like a grown-up, no matter how old we are, just doesn't come easy to us.

Kids do things that make their parents crazy. And parents do things that make their kids crazy. And this all happens in perfectly normal families. In other words, everybody in the family can be going crazy, but the family itself can seem perfectly normal. That's how crazy things are these days.

But I think I know how to make the world a better place. Here's my idea: Kids learn how to act in the world by watching how grown-ups act in the world. I don't think the world can ever get better unless this changes. We must make grown-ups act differently. And if the grown-ups will not cooperate, we will just have to put warning stickers on the ones who are not suitable for kids to be around. And that's the truth!

NIGHT TRAIN TO BOLINA

BY NILO CRUZ

TALITA, *14, has been living in a mission, waiting for her stepmother to come and take her to America.* SHE *speaks to Clara, also in her early teens, who has run away from her village with her boyfriend to the city (he stays in another part of the hospice, and they want to be with each other again).*

SCENE

At a convent in Latin America; two beds are on the stage.

TIME

The present.

TALITA: (*Runs to the door and sees if the nun has left.*) She'll be back later. She's Sister Nora. She's nice. When I can't sleep, because I have bad dreams, she tells me bedtime stories. Except she always falls asleep, instead of me. Then she starts snoring.

One time she took us to the zoo and I saw a monkey called Nunu. He was sitting like this. (*Sits on Clara's bed and crosses her legs.*) Like a little man with his legs crossed. He wasn't a boy. He was a woman. Not a woman. A monkey mother. Her little monkey was sleeping and she came to me and looked into my eyes like this. (*Moves her head from side to side.*) Then she went like this with her lips. (*Makes monkey sounds, does monkey movements and spins around.*)

[CLARA: (*Laughs.*) Do it again.]

TALITA: Good. I made you laugh. ([*Clara becomes serious again.*] TALITA *repeats motions.*) The little monkey would put her hand to her nose, like if she was going to sneeze. Like if she had a cold. Like this. (*Places hand on her nose, breathes in and out through her mouth and spins. Laughs.*) She looked like she wanted to be my mother. (*Pause. Faces forward.*) I don't have a mother. I used to have two mothers. I used to. Not anymore. One lives in America and one disappeared from home. My papi says she was kidnapped by soldiers. Do you know what kidnap means? [(*Clara shakes her head.*)] It means that they steal you. The soldiers that come to our village, they come and do bad things. They put people in bags of rice and take them away. Then they throw them into a pit.

Were you at the Santa Rosa Mission? [(*Clara shakes her head.*)] That's where my father took me, so my American mother can come for me. I'm going to be her daughter.

If I show you a secret, promise not to tell anybody. [(*Clara nods.*)] Stand there and close your eyes. I don't want anybody to know where I hide my secret. Come on, close your eyes and stand there. Go on over there. ([*Clara closes her eyes and walks away from* TALITA.] TALITA *pulls out a bundle from under her bed cushion.*) Open your eyes. And don't tell anybody I showed these to you. (TALITA *takes out a pair of shoes from inside a pillowcase.*) My mother in America sent them to me in a letter. In a little box. They didn't fit me when I got them. So my mother gave them to my sister, because she had bigger feet. Now they are small on me, because my feet got big. Try them on. They'll fit you. You have small feet. [(*Clara tries them on.*)] Aren't they beautiful.

But you see my sister scratched them. She never took care of them. She was going to break them and get them dirty, so I took them away from her. She was sleeping one night and I took them from under the bed. I put them inside a sack, I dug a hole and buried them inside the ground, so she wouldn't wear them again. Wait. Let me see if someone's coming. (*Runs to the door and takes a peek.* SHE *runs back to Clara.*) The next day everybody in my house was looking for the shoes. And I didn't tell. I didn't say anything. I used to go out at night and dig them out of the ground and wear them for a little while. Even if they were big on me. Then I would polish them with my nightshirt and dab a bit of saliva to make them shine. They would shine so much you could see the bright moon reflected on them. Go see if someone's coming. [(*Clara goes to the door.*)]

[CLARA: No one's out there.]

TALITA: She'll make her rounds again. Then she'll sit by the door and fall asleep. Let me wear the shoes.

NO SUCH COLD THING

BY NAOMI WALLACE

ALYA, 13, is an Afghan, hoping to go to England to live with her family. Her anticipation regarding her journey is hallucinatory, however; SHE is never able to escape the ravages of the war in her country.

SCENE

At the edge of a possible desert, near Kabul, Afghanistan.

TIME

Late autumn, 2001.

ALYA: Fauzia was walking with her father to see family. It was two years ago. She had on her best shoes and they made a click, click, click. Not loud but too loud. The Virtue Police heard Fauzia clicking and they shot her.

[(ALYA *watches Meena walk. Then Meena stops "clicking."*)]

It's true. Now you are prettier than she was.

[MEENA: Let's go.]

ALYA: We've been alone, Mother and I, and outside, the Taliban. We cannot leave the house. Mother had to stop her teaching; she is forbidden to work. Uncle Khan keeps us alive with scraps from his table. Our cousin Nargis laughed too loud at the market and the Police hit her and now she is missing three front teeth and is ugly. Girls are not allowed to go outside at all. I'm forbidden to learn to read and write. There is no one to collect the water. Uncle brings it. And all this. All this and you and Father are far away in England, clicking.

[MEENA: The plan was for Father and I to get out first. You know that. We couldn't get back here 'til now.]

ALYA: (*Calmly.*) Pig. I want to slap you.

[(*Meena steps close to* ALYA, *within her reach.*)

MEENA: Then slap me.

(*The two sisters just regard one another.*)]

ALYA: Does it rain in England all the time?

[MEENA: It rains. But it's not hard rain.

ALYA: Then Allah doesn't like England.] Will you take me to buy earrings?

[MEENA: Yes.]

ALYA: Mother says they have hedgehogs there. But with little ears, not like here with the long ears.

[MEENA: You can buy a bird at a shop on the high street and teach it to sit on your finger. You can't do that here.]

ALYA: Do the English like their hedgehogs?

[MEENA: There is a hedgehog society. You can join.]

ALYA: [But] they'll laugh at me. All the children in the new school will laugh at me.

ONCE AND FOR ALL WE'RE GONNA TELL YOU WHO WE ARE SO SHUT UP AND LISTEN

SCENARIO AND TEXT BY
ALEXANDER DEVRIENDT AND JOERI SMET

Just after the 13-member teenage cast creates an onstage mess (they are lying down during the monologue), NATHALIE, *15, independent and defiant, speaks directly to the audience.*

SCENE
A room with mismatched chairs, in Belgium, or anywhere.

TIME
The present.

NATHALIE: Let me be
Please
Let me be
You can ask all sorts of things from me
you can tell me what to do and what not to do
at what time I have to be home
you can do all that, I don't care...
But I will be home late
whatever hour you give me
I will pass that limit

and I will be completely wasted
and I will not be ashamed of myself
I have no choice, you see?
I have to go too far…
The moment that some of you are thinking:
"Does she have to?"
"Does she really have to do what she's doing?"
Yes, I do,
Okay?
Because I need to go further, a lot further,
until I don't know what to do anymore
and it's not because you've been there and done that
that I shouldn't go there and do that
because everything has been done before
but not by me
not now.

THE OUTCAST

BY BRENDA ROSS

SELA, *14, has run away from home to Clementine Hills, Florida, where* SHE *lives on the streets. But when* SHE *walks into a store called "Fantasia,"* SHE *discovers a world* SHE *never imagined. But how will it change her life?*

SCENE

Clementine Hills, Florida.

TIME

This moment.

SELA: I had run away from home, and I'd been living in the town of Clementine Hills, Florida, for a couple of days and nights when I saw the store. It had a giant purple sign that said "Fantasia" in big pink letters. I was really tired, 'cause sleeping on the sidewalk can really mess you up, and the only thing I could think was, "I could work here. Work means money. Money means bus ticket, bus ticket means getting out of here!" I didn't even see the sign that said "Sorry, we're closed," I just pushed the door open and stumbled inside. But the store was an empty dump! The only thing in the whole place besides me was a dirty couch, sitting in a corner, looking lonely. Right when I was about to leave, I stopped myself. A couch is sort of like a bed, and I thought that maybe I could sleep on the dusty couch instead of out on the sidewalk. The only problem was that I was worried that someone might come in and see me sleeping there. But I thought they wouldn't look in the storage room, so I decided to check that out and see if I could drag the couch in there. I opened the door that said "Supply Room: Employees Only" and gasped.

My eyes widened, my mouth dropped open and the only thing I could think or say was, "Wow." There were fairies flying everywhere, laughing and waving little silver wands. Real fairies! There were lots of small huts and houses made out of leaves and flowers. There were mini stores, schools, libraries, and super markets. It was full of nature and magic, and sitting in the center of it all was the prettiest fairy of them all, a brunette with big turquoise eyes, a gold wand, and a beautiful crown. She was perched on top of a throne, staring at me. It seemed like the moment I opened the door, everyone there turned and stared at me. I heard one fairy child whisper, "Is she human?" And another said, "Cool!" Then I saw a redheaded fairy in a lime-green dress whisper something to the brunette wearing the crown. "Well, Apple, there's really only one thing we can do. She has to become a fairy, too." The red-headed fairy, Apple, looked shocked by what she had heard. So was I. There never seemed to be a place for me in the human world. Would it be any different here? Or would I still be an outcast?

THE PERMIAN EXTINCTION

BY CATHERINE CASTELLANI

SOPHIA, *9, is practicing her report for science (*SHE*'s very serious about her work). The subject is the Permian Extinction, and the report will be delivered tomorrow.*

SCENE

SOPHIA*'s bedroom, which* SHE *has decorated with stars on the ceiling and a fake tree* SHE *has made of paper towel and bathroom tissue cardboard tubes.*

TIME

Evening.

SOPHIA: (SHE *practices in front of her Younger Brother.*) The Permian Extinction! By Sophia the Science Girl! This is scary, so listen. This is a horror story of the Earth's early days. Way in the back-back, before old-fashioned times, before the long-ago, in the time of the dinosaurs. Once upon a time, just about everything, or at least a whole lot of plants and animals…DIED. Just went extinct. And no one knows why!!! Like…maybe there were volcanoes? And the Earth might have just cracked open and dinosaurs fell in, and out came a gas, a bad gas called methane. It smelled like a dead egg all over the land. It smelled so bad all the leaves turned brown and curled up and DIED. It was *poison* that methane gas! That's one theory. Or an asteroid hit the Earth. Or so many volcanoes at once went off that the Earth was covered in *vog*. That's a real word. They have it in Hawaii: *vog*. It's volcanic smog! And it's real. And it's deadly. And it's Permian. Or it was. It could have been. It might even happen again! Today! (SHE *starts to bow, then realizes something.*) Wait, wait! I'm not done yet! Here's the good news: The Earth is a lot more geologically stable than it was back then, so don't worry too much about a big crazy eruption. Worry about outer space! Galaxies colliding! Meteor showers! Solar flares! ALIENS! I'll tell you all about the Milky Way versus Andromeda, next week on...Sophia the Science Girl! Okay. I'm done. Now you can clap.

PRETTY FOR AN ASIAN GIRL

BY LUCY WANG

MABEL, *a 13- to 14-year-old Asian-American girl, feels lucky* SHE *gets paid to tutor the most popular, best-looking boy in high school, until he pays her a compliment.*

SCENE
MABEL*'s bedroom.*

TIME
This moment.

MABEL: He said I was pretty for an Asian girl. And like a total idiot, I giggled and said thank you. I know, I'm pretty stupid when it comes to guys. Make that super stupid. I know how to get A's, but that's about it. But, hey, it was enough to get Trevor to ask me to be his personal tutor. Actually, his parents pay me. By the hour. Do you know how many girls would love to tutor Trevor? For free. I wanted to offer, but my mom and dad wouldn't let me do it for free. We need the money. We always need the money. Besides, they said it wouldn't be right, me wasting all that valuable time with a dumb boy. Dumb boy? Try the most wanted boy at Kucinich High. Seriously. He's so handsome. Popular. Athletic. It's really hard to concentrate when he flashes that smile. When his knees knock into yours. When he's staring back at you with those doey-eyes, full of mischief and wonder. Of course, it's not always dreamy. Sometimes you just want to scream or tear your hair out, how can he not know 6 times 7 is 42? Sometimes you run out of explanations. Words. Logic. But that's Trevor's gift, he senses when you're lost or stuck, and breaks right through. "You're so smart, Mabel. I bet you're going to be a brain surgeon. Me, I'm more of a brain donor," he said. I couldn't believe he said that about himself! (*A beat.*)

Today, he showed me a trick, how to get a shaker of salt to stand on one lonely salt crystal. It looked like it was going to fall, (SHE *tilts her body*) all tilted to one side, but it didn't. Aren't you impressed? I was. I'd never think of doing something like that. My parents are into order. (SHE *gestures tall, straight and narrow.*) "So Mabel," he asked, "do your parents tell you you're pretty?" Pretty? Did he say pretty or pity? My heart was racing so fast I couldn't hear. "Yeah, very pretty," he said. Trevor pointed that sharp Number 2 pencil at me. My face felt really hot so I played with my hair, like those girls in the movies, and I moved in closer because I thought he might want to kiss me, and I wanted to make it easier. That's when he said, "Very pretty for an Asian Girl." Thank you, thank you, but pretty for an Asian Girl, what does that mean? Was it a joke? I pulled back. I tossed and turned all night. Then the next day I raised my rates, and Trevor's parents said they couldn't afford me. I thought my parents were going to kill me for losing the job. But they didn't. They thought I was getting too boy-crazy, too easily distracted. I guess they were right.

THE RIMERS OF ELDRITCH

BY LANFORD WILSON

EVA JACKSON *is a crippled girl, 14. Here, before* SHE *is attacked,* SHE *is walking in the woods with her friend Robert, a boy of 18 (who is small and quiet).*

SCENE

Eldritch, a small former mining town in the Middle West; population about 70.

TIME

The '60s.

EVA: Don't you wish it was autumn? Don't you? Don't you love autumn? And the wind and rime and pumpkins and gourds and corn shocks?...Don't you love autumn? Don't you, Robert? I won't call you that. Everybody else does but I won't.

[ROBERT: I haven't thought about it.]

EVA: [Well,] think about it, right now. Think about how it smells.

[ROBERT: How does it smell?]

EVA: [Like] dry, windy, cold, frosty rime and chaff and leaf smoke and corn husks.

[ROBERT: It does, huh?]

EVA: Pretend. Close your eyes. Are your eyes closed? Don't you wish it was here? Like apples and cider... [You go].

[ROBERT: And rain.]

EVA: [Sometimes.] And potatoes and flower seeds and honey...

[ROBERT: And popcorn and butter.

EVA: (*Opening her eyes.*) [Yes. Oh, it does not!] You're not playing at all. There's hay and clover and alfalfa and all that...

[Continuing...]

EVA: [No,] in the winter time and in the autumn. It's so nice, it smells so clean.

[ROBERT: (*Circles...* EVA *following.*) Okay, the fall then.]

EVA: (*Stops.*) [Yes.] And it's heavy, heavy frost and it covers every thing and that's rime.

[ROBERT: And it's just frost? Is it a hoarfrost?]

EVA: [That's it,] hoarfrost is rime. And it covers everything. Every little blade of grass and every tree and houses and everything. Like it's been dipped in water and then in sugar.

[ROBERT: Or salt. Yeah, I know what it is.]

EVA: It's better than ice storms or anything like that. And everything is white and sparkling so clean when the sun comes up it nearly blinds you and it's rare! It doesn't happen every year. And that's what I'd like to be. What I'd like to do. I have a book with a picture of Jack Frost painting rime on a window pane with a paint brush. Do you fly? Do you dream you fly?

[ROBERT: When?]

EVA: Ever?

[ROBERT: I guess. I haven't thought about it.]

EVA: How high? Think about it. It's important. Everybody flies, it's important how high.

[ROBERT: I don't know. Just over the ground.

EVA: Really?

ROBERT: I guess. As high as my head. I'm always getting tangled up in wires and all.]

EVA: I'm way over the tree tops, just over the tree tops, just brushing against the tree tops, and I fly right over them, just brush them with my arms out. Over the whole town like an airplane. Spreading this salt frost in the autumn. I love autumn. And when the sun comes—

[ROBERT: Right.]

EVA: It'll blind you!

[ROBERT: I've seen it.]

EVA: It's so bright it blinds you. I want to fly like that, all over the town, right over everybody. It's beautiful. Listen. Listen. Did you hear something?

ROMEO AND JULIET
BY WILLIAM SHAKESPEARE

JULIET, *14, speaks of her love for Romeo, contemplating the division created by their warring families.*

SCENE
JULIET*'s high window, Capulet's orchard in Verona, Italy.*

TIME
In the 14th or 15th century—or wherever your mind might take you.

JULIET: O Romeo, Romeo! wherefore art thou Romeo?
Deny thy father and refuse thy name;
Or, if thou wilt not, be but sworn my love,
And I'll no longer be a Capulet.

[ROMEO: (*Aside.*) Shall I hear more, or shall I speak at this?]

JULIET: 'Tis but thy name that is my enemy;
Thou art thyself, though not a Montague.
What's Montague? it is nor hand, nor foot,
Nor arm, nor face, nor any other part
Belonging to a man. O, be some other name!
What's in a name? that which we call a rose
By any other name would smell as sweet;
So Romeo would, were he not Romeo call'd,

Retain that dear perfection which he owes
Without that title. Romeo, doff thy name,
And for that name which is no part of thee
Take all myself.

ROMEO AND JULIET
BY WILLIAM SHAKESPEARE

JULIET, *14, waits for her Nurse, who is acting as a messenger, to return, bringing wedding plans from Romeo.*

SCENE
Verona, Italy, in Capulet's orchard.

TIME
The 14th or 15th century—or wherever love is young.

JULIET: The clock struck nine when I did send the nurse;
In half an hour she promised to return.
Perchance she cannot meet him: that's not so.
O, she is lame! love's heralds should be thoughts,
Which ten times faster glide than the sun's beams,
Driving back shadows over louring hills:
Therefore do nimble-pinion'd doves draw love,
And therefore hath the wind-swift Cupid wings.
Now is the sun upon the highmost hill
Of this day's journey, and from nine till twelve
Is three long hours, yet she is not come.
Had she affections and warm youthful blood,
She would be as swift in motion as a ball;
My words would bandy her to my sweet love,
And his to me:

But old folks, many feign as they were dead;
Unwieldy, slow, heavy and pale as lead.
O God, she comes!

[(*Enter Nurse and Peter.*)]

O honey nurse, what news?
Hast thou met with him? Send thy man away.

ROMEO AND JULIET

BY WILLIAM SHAKESPEARE

JULIET, *14, waits impatiently for night to come, when* SHE *will see Romeo. Instead, the Nurse arrives bringing word that* JULIET*'s cousin Tybalt is dead and Romeo, banished.*

SCENE

Capulet's house, Verona, Italy.

TIME

The 14th or 15th century—or whenever there are young lovers.

JULIET: Gallop apace, you fiery-footed steeds,
Towards Phoebus' lodging: such a wagoner
As Phaethon would whip you to the west,
And bring in cloudy night immediately.
Spread thy close curtain, love-performing night,
That runaway's eyes may wink and Romeo
Leap to these arms, untalk'd of and unseen.
Lovers can see to do their amorous rites
By their own beauties; or, if love be blind,
It best agrees with night. Come, civil night,
Thou sober-suited matron, all in black,
And learn me how to lose a winning match,
Play'd for a pair of stainless maidenhoods:
Hood my unmann'd blood, bating in my cheeks,

With thy black mantle; till strange love, grown bold,
Think true love acted simple modesty.
Come, night; come, Romeo; come, thou day in night;
For thou wilt lie upon the wings of night
Whiter than new snow on a raven's back.
Come, gentle night, come, loving, black-brow'd night,
Give me my Romeo; and, when he shall die,
Take him and cut him out in little stars,

And he will make the face of heaven so fine
That all the world will be in love with night
And pay no worship to the garish sun.
O, I have bought the mansion of a love,
But not possess'd it, and, though I am sold,
Not yet enjoy'd: so tedious is this day
As is the night before some festival
To an impatient child that hath new robes
And may not wear them. O, here comes my nurse,
And she brings news; and every tongue that speaks
But Romeo's name speaks heavenly eloquence.

[(*Enter Nurse, with cords.*)]

Now, nurse, what news? What hast thou there? the cords
That Romeo bid thee fetch?

THE SEARCH FOR SIGNS OF INTELLIGENT LIFE IN THE UNIVERSE

WRITTEN BY JANE WAGNER AND
PERFORMED BY LILY TOMLIN

AGNUS ANGST *is an articulate and rebellious teenager who is ruminating about all the things* SHE *finds wrong with the world* SHE *lives in.*

SCENE
AGNUS ANGST*'s home.*

TIME
Today.

AGNUS ANGST: I'm Agnus Angst!
I don't kiss ass; I don't say thanks.
I'm getting my act together and throwing it in your face.
I want to insult every member of the human race.
Even as a fetus, I had womb angst. I knew that the world I was coming into was liable
To be a 'pins-in-girl-scout-cookies', gun obsessed, porno-strewn, kick-box-culture.
I don't want to go, please! I don't want to go!

What's coming up for me is something from my own soap
opera.
I look at my family, and I feel like a detached retina.
The last really deep conversation I had with my Dad was
between our T-shirts.
His said, "Science is Truth Found Out."
Mine said, "The Truth Can Be Made Up If You Know How."

When I was leaving for the *Un*-Club one night, my mother
said,
"As long as you're going out, take out the trash."
I looked around the room–at her seashells shadow box and her
imitation Early American maple coffee table in the shape
of a wagon wheel and her salt and pepper shaker collection.
I see the wrought-iron lamppost with a ceramic drunk
leaning against it.
"Take out the *trash*?" I wouldn't know *where* to begin.

On the radio, I heard the weatherman say,
"The air today is unacceptable. People with breathing problems
should not go out."
I wanted to shout,
"What's unacceptable is that the *air* is unacceptable!"
I think: Wow, breathing is a bio-hazard–if we don't take in air
every few minutes, we die; but the air we're taking in is
killing us.

My new guru is Gordon Liddy, who, when holding his hand
over a lit candle, said,
"The trick is not to mind it."
I didn't mind it when I heard that Ozzy Osbourne bit the head
of a bat.

And I don't mind no matter how much contempt I have for
society,
It's nothing compared to the contempt society has for me.
Last year there was a shooting at school. I watched my teacher
get blown away.
She was the only one who ever gave me an "A"
And she got a bullet not an apple that day.
But I didn't mind it.

I don't mind that I took my goldfish and I put it in water from
the faucet
and it died, and our drinking water caused it.
I tried my mouth-to-mouth resuscitation skills.
My dad said, "You are the daughter of a scientist–
it should have been mouth-to-gills."
But I don't mind it.

I don't mind each morning I get up, I feel like I want to throw
up.
I don't mind that my parents, all four of them, are narcissists
who refuse to grow up.
And I don't mind that the boy in school who I love the most
died last year of an overdose.
I want my skin to thicken so if I am panic-stricken when the
greenhouse effect is here,
I won't feel the fear as I watch me and the human race
disappear.

The trick is not to mind it.
If you're looking for peace, here is where you'll find it.
Gordon Liddy showed me the way.
Life is like the candle flame, and we are the hand hovering over
it.

It hurts like hell, but the trick is not to mind it.
I mind it! I mind it!

*As an FBI agent, Gordon Liddy planned and supervised the Democratic National Committee break-in at the Watergate complex in 1972. He later became a radio talk show host and died in 2012.

SEEING THE INVISIBLE

BY MICHAEL EDAN

A 12- to14-year-old GIRL *is talking to her best friend while looking at the stars.*

SCENE
Outside in nature.

TIME
Night. The present.

GIRL: Well, you can laugh at me all you want and say how I'm just acting like a kid and need to grow up, but I do believe in magic because I've seen it. This summer we went to visit my grandparents, you know who have the farm, and there was something I saw that was soooooo cool. It was early evening and we had just finished a hot dog roast and my grandmother took me on a walk. We're looking over this huge field. Mugwort. That's what it was. She said it was named after the lunar goddess Artemis and had magical properties. Like they use it in dream pillows. And the Native Americans believe that rubbing mugwort leaves on the body will keep ghosts away. (*Pause.*) Well, that's what they say. I didn't make it up! Anyway that's not the point of the story. So we're looking over this large field of mugwort, and it's a full moon, and it's all really beautiful. Then we notice all across the field there are these twinkling lights...you know fireflies. And it was amazing because they were all over the place, like hundreds and hundreds of them. And we're just standing there, silent, watching these thousands of fireflies twinkling. And then the strangest thing happened. I don't know how to explain it, but I could see this pattern in the lights, and they were somehow all connected, like some kind of grid that was a code, a code that was expressed through the blinking of the lights. You're looking at me like I'm crazy, but I'm telling you it was like a language being shown to me, a mathematical language. And its message was how the fireflies, and the field, and the sky, and me were all connected. And then it went away. I couldn't see it anymore. But I knew I had seen it. Something that's usually invisible. My grandmother thought it was one of the languages of God. I don't know about that. But it sure was magical.

SHAWNA

BY SOFIA DUBRAWSKY

SHAWNA, *13-14, is currently battling cancer.* SHE *is at a summer camp designed for teens in treatment. Her cabin is performing a ceremony, and it is* SHAWNA*'s turn to share. The group stands in a circle.* SHAWNA *holds a stick, a rock, and a shell in her hands.*

SCENE
The beach.

TIME
Night, the present.

SHAWNA: This stick represents cancer....I'm ready to let it go forever....(SHE *throws the stick into the ocean.*) This rock represents my fear, the nightmare I keep having. It's, I'm—I'm lying on this big table, but actually it isn't a table, it's more like a hospital bed, maybe, I'm not sure but I can't move and it's really cold. Everyone is around me: my mom, my sister, Dr. Kelston and the nurses. And they are all staring down at me, smiling, laughing, and they are talking to each other, like they're having a party. And they are eating something weird, pink, and red. They are stuffing their mouths and their cheeks are all greasy, and they're licking their lips and fingers like it's chicken but it's not. I try to talk to them but they don't hear me. And then I look down and see there is a hole in my belly and they are reaching in with their hands and pulling out pieces of my body and eating me! Scooping their hands in and pulling out parts of me! I start screaming, "Stop! Stop it!" but they don't stop, they don't even hear me. Then I look down further and see my legs are gone. I just have these two stumps left. Then my mom suddenly barges forward, she grabs the biggest handful of all and laughs really loud. I see my insides all around, chunks of pink, red meat and organs falling everywhere, and people are just smacking their mouths and teeth, grinning down at me! I look down again and the hole looks empty. I'm almost gone! I force myself to wake up. This rock is that dream, and I never want to have it again! (SHE *throws the rock as far as* SHE *can.*)...And this shell represents the new friends that I made this summer; I picked the shell for my friends because it's beautiful. I found it down there near the driftwood and I'm going to keep it with me forever. Yes, forever.

12 OPHELIAS (A PLAY WITH BROKEN SONGS)

BY CARIDAD SVICH

OPHELIA *(from Shakespeare's* HAMLET*), 13 years old—and simultaneously ageless—finds herself in a new world in this play. Here,* SHE *speaks to a young woman named Mina, defending and rebelling against her path through history.*

SCENE
In a field in the Appalachians.

TIME
Fluid: past and present. Mythic time.

OPHELIA: I forget things. Slowly.
Even drowning is in the past.
Crushed daises in my hands
and long purple stems at my feet.
A picture only. A portrait of another century
hanging on a wall in a museum.
That was me. I point at the picture and smile,
pleased at my forgetting,
and a-comin' back to where Jesus wept,
and He wept, didn't he?
That's another story, but it's felt here on earth,
in this land, as we reach to heaven;

we feel weeping,
and sad tales of girls wronged
and left with broken families, and oh how we weep, pitchers
full, jars full, wells of weeping,
but it don't mean anything.
Not to the girl. Not to the woman.
So, she returns, unmasks herself,
takes off the fresh flowered look
and replaces it with something true,
something real she can offer now,
cause she's cried and lost things,
she's an earned being;
and earning has value to the soul.
It makes a difference now that she's on land
and walking and not a-fearing herself anymore,
even if the rude boy is rude; this she knows,
she's lived it before, and she's ready again.
Tell me what I don't know,
and I'll spin you a tale of woe
that will break your iron heart
and leave it on the floor.
Stick me with a hundred branches. I'll heal.

TO BE YOUNG, GIFTED AND BLACK: A PORTRAIT OF LORRAINE HANSBERRY IN HER OWN WORDS

ADAPTED BY ROBERT NEMIROFF

LORRAINE HANSBERRY, *13 or older, relates the games of her childhood.*

SCENE
The South Side of Chicago.

TIME
In the '30s, early '40s, or wherever you had the most fun playing with your friends.

LORRAINE: [My childhood] South Side summers were the ordinary city kind, full of the street games and rhymes that anticipated what some people insist on calling modern poetry: (*Listens a moment, reaching back into memory, and suddenly plucks the words to the tune out of the air and begins to sing:*)

Oh Mary, Mack, Mack, Mack
All dressed in black, black, black—
With the silver buttons, buttons, buttons
All down her back, back, back—
She asked her mother, mother, mother—

For fifty cents, cents, cents
To see the elephant, elephant, elephant
Jump the fence, fence, fence.
Well, he jumped so high, high, high
'Til he touched the sky, sky, sky
And he didn't come back, back, back
'Til the Fourth of July, ly, ly!

[I remember] skinny little South Side bodies by the fives and tens of us, panting the delicious hours away:

(*Eagerly straining forward* [*and vying with each other to be chosen*].)

May I?

And the voice of authority:

(*Playing the Leader.*) "Yes…you—(*Suspensefully surveying the group with a finger.*) MAY—!

[(Points and the favored GIRL steps forward into position.)] You may take—One—giant—STEP! One—giant—STEP! One—giant—STEP!

One drew in all one's breath and tightened one's fist and pulled the small body against the heavens, stretching, straining all the muscles in the legs, to make—one…giant…step. (*Savoring the moment.*) It is a long time. One forgets. Why was it important to take a small step, a teeny step, or—one giant step? (*Thoughtful pause.*) A giant step to *where?*

TO BE YOUNG, GIFTED AND BLACK: A PORTRAIT OF LORRAINE HANSBERRY IN HER OWN WORDS

ADAPTED BY ROBERT NEMIROFF

LORRAINE HANSBERRY, *13 or older, talks about summer and her dad.*

SCENE
The South Side of Chicago in the summer.

TIME
Evening.

LORRAINE: Evenings were spent mainly on the back porches where screen doors slammed in the darkness with those really very special summertime sounds. (SHE *listens and smiles, transported,* [*as the singer begins to sing. After his second "O Lord, man, you can't come in,"* SHE *resumes and the music fades under and slowly out.*]) And sometimes, when Chicago nights got too steamy, we would go out to the park where it was cool and sweet to be on the grass and there was usually the scent of freshly cut lemons or melons in the air. Daddy would lie on his back, as fathers must, and explain about how men thought the stars above us came to be and how far away they were. (*With a touch of wonder.*) I never did learn to believe that anything could be as far away as *that*. Especially… the stars.

TO BE YOUNG, GIFTED AND BLACK: A PORTRAIT OF LORRAINE HANSBERRY IN HER OWN WORDS

ADAPTED BY ROBERT NEMIROFF

LORRAINE HANSBERRY, *13 or older, talks about the death of a young man in New York.*

SCENE
A Harlem church in the middle of the 20th century.

TIME
Before a funeral.

LORRAINE: Harlem church, a Baptist church. It's not a Sunday and nobody is dressed up. People out on the sidewalk in front of the church ask: "Who is it?" And nobody with an angry face whispers the answer. When you go in, it's quiet. Nobody is crying. It's just quiet. And then we wait. You think while you wait. The church reminds you of all the Sundays you have ever known. Soap and flower odors...and music. Most of all it reminds of music...And you wait. Somebody asks: "Why haven't they come? What is wrong?" And the Minister says there has been a delay, but they are coming now. And then you go up close to the long copper-colored box and look in it. (*A very slight inaudible gasp.* SHE *scans the coffin.*) He was very big. He was handsome and his face still looks kind. You can't see his fists, they are under that part which is closed, but you get the feeling that they are balled up tight. (*Stands looking for a long moment. Then:*) You stand watching him a long time. And an old woman comes and stands beside you and she asks you, "What was wrong with him, such a strong young man?" You tell her he was killed, shot. (*Half knowing the answer even as* SHE *asks—with the deep, quiet bitterness of a lifetime rather than explosive anger.*) "The cops," she asks, "did a cop do it?" And you say, yes it was a cop. And she shakes her head. "He is very *young,*" she says. And she looks at him and she looks at you. And she says— (*Idiomatically, with resignation.*) I guess it don't make no difference about going to school then." And you—are quiet. (*Takes a last look, stops, reaches out as if to touch the coffin, then exits.*)

TO BE YOUNG, GIFTED AND BLACK: A PORTRAIT OF LORRAINE HANSBERRY IN HER OWN WORDS

ADAPTED BY ROBERT NEMIROFF

LORRAINE HANSBERRY, *11 or older, recalls a trip with her family.*

SCENE
The South.

TIME
Summer.

LORRAINE: My mother first took us south to visit her Tennessee birthplace one summer when I was seven or eight. I woke up while we were still driving through some place called Kentucky and my mother was pointing out to the beautiful hills and telling my brothers about how *her* father had run away and hidden from his master in those very hills when he was a little boy. (*With the child's recollected fear and wonder at the mystery and adventure of it.*) She said that his mother had wandered among the wooded slopes in the moonlight and left food for him in secret places. They were very beautiful hills and I looked out at them for miles and miles after that, wondering *who* and *what* a "master" might be. (*Smiling fondly and perhaps chuckling.*) I remember being startled when I first saw my grandmother rocking away on her porch. *All* my life I had heard that she was a great beauty—but no one had ever remarked that they meant a half century before! The woman that *I* met was as wrinkled as a prune and could hardly hear and barely see and always seemed to be thinking of other times. But she could still rock and talk and even make wonderful cupcakes—[(*To the Others.*)] which were like cornbread, only sweet. She died the next summer and that is all that I remember about her, except that she was born into slavery and had memories of it and—(*Flavorfully and idiomatically.*) they didn't sound anything like—(*Broadly satirizing it.*) *Gone with the Wind*!

TWO STEPS FROM THE STARS

BY JEAN-ROCK GAUDREAULT

MAGGIE, *11-12, has started a rumor at school that* SHE *is in love with her friend Junior (he doesn't know yet), who would like to be an astronaut.* SHE *would like to become a journalist.* MAGGIE *also thinks that her mother, sister, and her cousin are pretty—but not her.* SHE *wants to be popular.*

SCENE
On the way home from school.

TIME
Afternoon.

MAGGIE: I want to be pretty so that people know I exist.

[JUNIOR: But you do exist, Magpie, otherwise I'm completely crazy. Besides, someone can exist even if no one knows it.]

MAGGIE: [But] it feels awful. When I walk into the classroom, I feel like I'm invisible. Nobody says hello. The teacher takes attendance, he calls out my name, and I exist for a few seconds: I answer: present. Then I disappear among all the others.

[JUNIOR: You could stand up and shout: I'm here. I exist.]

MAGGIE: [I don't dare,] I'm shy, I can't help it. There's nothing special about me. I have a big sister and a little brother—I'm in the middle. At school, I'm not the best in the class or the worst—I'm average. When we walk in a line, I'm not the tallest or the shortest, I walk in the centre. The house I live in is neither pretty nor ugly—there are lots of others that look just like it. My parents aren't rich, they aren't poor. I'm not unhappy, so I should be happy. You see, there's nothing in between. You either laugh or you cry. And my problem is I'm not too unhappy, and I'm not happy enough.

THE WILD DUCK

BY HENRIK IBSEN

HEDVIG, *14, does not go to school due to her failing eyesight. Instead, when* SHE*'s allowed,* SHE *helps her parents with her father's photography business (he's an inventor, as well).* HEDVIG *also works taking care of rabbits, pigeons, and other animals, including a maimed wild duck, who live in her family's attic. Here, her father leaves the family, having found out that* SHE *may not be his real child.* HEDVIG, *who is symbolized by the wild duck, tries to figure out the best way to show how much he means to her.*

SCENE

Hjalmar Ekdal's apartment in Christiania, now Oslo, Norway.

TIME

The 1880s. HEDVIG*'s birthday.*

HEDVIG: (*Opening the kitchen door*) Father, father! What is that you're saying? No! No! Don't leave, please don't leave me! Mother, he's going away! He's going away from us!

(*Pause.*)

(*Sobbing on the sofa.*) This will kill me! He's not going to come back. Mother, you must get him. He's not coming back. He'll never come home anymore. What have I done to him? (*Weeping convulsively.*)

(*Silence.*)

(Sits up and dries her tears). He doesn't want me anymore, I can tell. Why doesn't Father want me? I can't go on like this....

(*Pause.*)

I'm not really father's child....That's what I think. Mother might have found me. Perhaps father knows; I've read stories like that....

(*Pause.*)

He still loves me no matter what, he must. Like the wild duck. The wild duck was given to us as a present, and, still, I love her so much!

(*Pause.*)

Father wanted to wring her neck! He doesn't want to see her anymore. I'm sure he doesn't mean it....I pray for the wild duck every night, and ask that she be protected from death and all evil.

(*Pause.*)

I taught myself to pray when father was sick, with leeches on his neck, and death stared him in the face. I prayed for him as I lay in bed...and I still do. The wild duck was so weak, too. I wanted to bring her in when she was found...so she could live in the attic with everything there: the big cupboards full of books....the big clock....She didn't have friends like the hens, who were chicks together....She's from the wild. Real. True. She belongs to me. My dearest treasure.

(*Silence.*)

Father didn't kill the wild duck because of me; he and grandfather built places for her and looked after her.

(*Silence.*)

(Rising). The wild duck! She belonged to me.

(*Pause.*)

In the morning....I'll ask grandfather to shoot her.

(*Pause.*)

Father will see how much I love him....I pray he'll see that....

PART TWO

MONOLOGUES FOR BOYS

ADVENTURES OF HUCKLEBERRY FINN

BY MARK TWAIN

Two con men, calling themselves a duke and a king—as well as Shakespearean actors—practice the bard; HUCKLEBERRY FINN, *about 13, watches and learns Hamlet's soliloquy.*

SCENE

Traveling down the Mississippi River on a raft.

TIME

After dinner, in 1839 or 1840.

HUCKLEBERRY: He told us to give attention. Then he [the duke] strikes a most noble attitude, with one leg shoved forwards, and his arms stretched away up, and his head tilted back, looking up at the sky; and then he begins to rip and rave and grit his teeth; and after that, all through his speech, he howled, and spread around, and swelled up his chest, and just knocked the spots out of any acting ever I see before. This is the speech—I learned it, easy enough, while he was learning it to the king:

To be, or not to be; that is the bare bodkin
That makes calamity of so long life;

For who would fardels bear, till Birnam Wood do come to
Dunsinane,
But that the fear of something after death
Murders the innocent sleep,
Great nature's second course,
And makes us rather sling the arrows of outrageous fortune
Than fly to others that we know not of.
There's the respect must give us pause:
Wake Duncan with thy knocking! I would thou couldst;
For who would bear the whips and scorns of time,
The oppressor's wrong, the proud man's contumely,
The law's delay, and the quietus which his pangs might take,
In the dead waste and middle of the night, when churchyards
yawn
In customary suits of solemn black,
But that the undiscovered country from whose bourne no
traveler returns,
Breathes forth contagion on the world,
And thus the native hue of resolution, like the poor cat i' the
adage,
Is sicklied o'er with care,
And all the clouds that lowered o'er our housetops,
With this regard their currents turn awry,
And lose the name of action.
'Tis a consummation devoutly to be wished.
But soft you, the fair Ophelia:
Ope not thy ponderous and marble jaws,
But get thee to a nunnery—go!

BAD DREAM

BY BERNARDO SOLANO
AND STEPHEN FIFE

A 12- to 14-year-old boy describes his crazy dreams, mulling over their meaning.

SCENE
Anywhere you choose.

TIME
The present.

MARIO: Okay, I'm in bed with rats all over me so I jump out and run to the bathroom and get in the shower. When I turn it on, fire and sparks shoot out and burn me, then suddenly I fall through the floor and keep falling till I get to Hell and I run into an elevator with the Devil chasing me. I get away, but it's midnight and a vampire kills all my friends and family. My best friend survives but he changes into a massive dog that attacks me, and I'm forced to hurt it out of self-defense. Then here comes Michael Myers with that mask and a chainsaw, so I jump across the Grand Canyon to get away and I…I wake up in another life. I'm an Afghan person and I'm looking for safety in the middle of a war. America is bombing us and I'm scared. I try to convince an American soldier that I'm him, that I'm an American, but he doesn't believe me. He points his gun at me and I…I wake up again. But this time I'm in my bed. My real bed. The rats are gone, the devil and the chainsaws are gone, too. I forget about all of them right away, but I can't stop thinking about that Afghan person. I think about him all day. And I wonder: Does he feel like he's in a bad dream? Does he close his eyes, hoping that when he opens them, he'll be in another life, at home in his bed?

BARKING SHARKS

BY ISRAEL HOROVITZ

LITTLE EDDIE, *a precocious young man of 13-14, remembers the summers* HE *spent with his parents on an island off the coast of France.*

SCENE

Gloucester, Massachusetts, where LITTLE EDDIE *is speaking to the audience.*

TIME

The present, talking about the past.

LITTLE EDDIE: We used'ta go to this island off the coast of France, every July, from the time I was five 'til, well, now. We had this little old farmhouse. My father used'ta spend all his time reading books on philosophy, in French. My mother used'ta to read about a thousand novels. My main job was to hang around and be quiet. I spent two Julys in a boys' sleep-over sports-camp in, uh, America, but, we don't talk about it. Otherwise, I was on this French island with my folks, every summer. I didn't exactly hate it. A lot of it was pretty nice, but, I never really knew many other kids there, and the language thing was tough for the first ten years or so. We did a lot of nice biking...beautiful beaches, and dealing with my father's bouts of Existential Malaise. He would worry about whether or not he really existed. Every day, until supper-time, then he'd eat oysters and worry about hepatitis. My father worries a lot.

¡BOCÓN!

BY LISA LOOMER

MIGUEL, *12, a "bocón" or "big mouth," stands in a courtroom. His parents have been taken by the army of a repressive regime, and* HE *is heading north after them. Shyly, awkwardly, gaining steam,* HE *answers a Judge.*

SCENE

In a Central American detention center, at the border.

TIME

The past...and the present, too.

MIGUEL: Señor—Judge, digo...You ask where I come from. Why I'm here. (*Begins awkwardly.*) Pos...Yo vengo de...es un pubelito...I come from a small village, San Juan de La Paz, in the middle of my country...by the river they call La Ballena—because the river swells up sometimes like a fat green whale! And we—all the people there work for Don Madera, picking his coffee for him in the fields and—(*Remembers; smiles.*) My father says he can't pick his own coffee 'cause his belly is so big, he (*Sticks his belly out.*) can't find the basket! (*Laughs at his joke—then explains it.*) To put the coffee beans in, pos...Bueno, after you're done working you could go to the Plaza—where there's always people selling... Pupusas! Bananos! Flores! Tamales! Aguacates! Y Firecrackers... Para La Fiesta de San Juan! The Saints love firecrackers, that's how they know there's a fiesta. (*To the sky.*) Saints—come down from the sky, and bring a fat juicy pig for Rosita! (*Suddenly scared.*) But there were soldiers in the plaza, too. And the soldiers didn't like us to shout—or sing. Or *dance*. If you danced, the soldiers could make you...disappear. Many people in my village...disappeared. (*Remembers; smiles.*) But there was an old Indian, Kiki El Loco, who used to dance all the time at fiestas—right in the plaza! They say he was deaf—but he could hear music right through the ground—like a radio! The people would tell him, "Kiki! Alli vienen los soldados, Kiki! The soldiers!" But Kiki—he'd just keep dancing! (MIGUEL *starts to dance himself now, stomping, insistent.*) Mira! The Dance of the Quetzal! The Bird of Freedom! (*Laughs.*) Kiki El Loco—he could dance the soldiers away! He's not afraid of nothing!

(*The monologue can end here. Or,* MIGUEL *then stops dancing.* HE *turns to the Judge, catching his breath.*)

MIGUEL: Señor—Judge, digo...Are you going to send me back? If you do, I'll just come back again...I'm not going to disappear.

DANNY THE CHAMPION OF THE WORLD

BY DAVID WOOD, ADAPTED FROM THE BOOK BY ROALD DAHL

DANNY, *9, is very close to his father, who runs a small garage.* DANNY*'s mother died a few years ago. Tonight,* HE *has woken up to find his dad missing (later, we find out that he has been poaching pheasants). Here,* DANNY *ponders the situation.*

SCENE
Outside, sitting on the steps.

TIME
The present.

DANNY: I don't get it. What's Dad up to? Where's he been? He left me on my own. Why won't he talk about it? He's never done it before! Maybe he *has*, and I've never woken up before! No, he wouldn't. Would he? Not Dad. He's a great dad. Since Mum died he's had to look after me all on his own, cook the meals, do the washing. He's a great dad, he really is. He teaches me things. Like grasshoppers have their ears, guess where?...in the sides of their tummies. But crickets have ears in their legs! He takes me hunting for birds' nests. We found a skylark's once, on the ground in a field, with six tiny eggs, all brown and white. But you mustn't touch them or their mother might abandon them. We made a kite out of some sticks and an old blue shirt. It's got a proper tail and a long string and it flies brilliantly, as long as the wind doesn't drop. Dad's great at making things. Last birthday he built me an amazing car out of bike wheels and old soapboxes. I whizz really fast on it, shooting down the hill. He's a great dad. He smiles with his eyes. All twinkly. You know how some people smile at you with their mouths (HE *demonstrates.*), but their eyes stay the same. That's not twinkly. Dad's twinkly. (*Pause.*) He wasn't so twinkly tonight, though. More like shifty.... What's he up to?

DON QUIXOTE

BY MIGUEL DE CERVANTES

ANDRÉS, *about 15, is running away from his master, a farmer, heading for Seville, Spain. On his journey,* HE *meets the knight Don Quixote, "the undoer of wrongs and injustices," for a second time. Their first encounter occurred as* ANDRÉS *is tied to an oak tree and whipped for failing to tend sheep properly—*ANDRÉS, *although probably guilty, protests that* HE *hadn't been paid for nine months. Before taking his leave, Don Quixote sides with the shepherd and insists that the salary be paid, angering the farmer even further. Now,* ANDRÉS *has rushed up to Don Quixote and clasped him around the legs, bursting into tears.*

SCENE

Near a spring, in the undistinguished countryside in Castile–La Mancha, Spain, on the road to Seville.

TIME

The 1590s.

ANDRÉS: (*Remembering.*) I won't do it again, master mine; by God's passion I won't do it again, and I'll take more care of the flock another time…(*To Don Quixote.*) Señor, he flogs me only because I ask for my wages…

This master of mine is not a knight, nor has he received any order of knighthood, for he is Juan Haldudo the Rich, of Quintanar... he refuses me the wages of my sweat and labor...I go with him! Nay, God forbid! No, señor, not for the world...once alone with me, he would ray me like a Saint Bartholomew...

(*In the present.*) O, señor, do you not know me? Look at me well; I am that lad Andrés that your worship released from the oak-tree where I was tied...

(*Pause.*)

...the end of the business turned out just the opposite of what your worship supposes...

(*Pause.*)

Not only did he not pay me...but as soon as your worship had passed out of the wood and we were alone, he tied me up again to the same oak and gave me a fresh flogging, that left me like a flayed Saint Bartholomew, and every stroke he gave me he followed up with some jest or gibe about having made a fool of your worship, and but for the pain I was suffering I should have laughed at the things he said. In short he left me in such a condition that I have been until now in a hospital getting cured of the injuries which that rascally clown inflicted on me then, for all which your worship is to blame; for if you had gone your own way and not come where there was no call for you, nor meddled in other people's affairs, my master would have been content with giving me one or two dozen lashes, and would have then loosed me and paid me what he owed me, but when your worship abused him so out of measure, and gave him so many hard words, his anger was kindled, and as he could not revenge himself on you, as soon as he saw you had left him, the storm burst upon me in such a way, that I feel as if I should never be a man again...

I have no faith in...oaths. I would rather have now something to help me to get to Seville than all the revenges in the world; if you have here anything to eat that I can take with me, give it me, and God be with your worship and all knights-errant, and may their errands turn out as well for themselves as they have for me.

(ANDRÉS *seizes a piece of bread and cheese. Pause.*)

For the love of God, sir knight-errant, if you ever meet me again, though you may see them cutting me to pieces, give me no aid or succor, but leave me to my misfortune, which will not be so great but that a greater will come to me by being helped by your worship, on whom—and all the knights-errant that have ever been born—God send his curse.

EXILES

BY JAMES JOYCE

In order to ride with the milkman in the morning, ARCHIE, *8, must get permission. This means* HE *has to convince his father—a writer named Richard—to talk to his mother. Before racing into the garden,* ARCHIE *explains how much* HE *wants to drive the milkcar and see the cows in the field. His family, recently returned to Ireland, has lived in Italy for 9 years.*

SCENE
Suburban Dublin.

TIME
Summer, 1912.

ARCHIE: [(*Plucks his father by the sleeve.*)] I say, pappie!

[RICHARD: (*Absently.*) What is it?]

ARCHIE: I want to ask you a thing.

[RICHARD: (*Sitting on the end of the lounge, stares in front of him.*) What is it?]

ARCHIE: Will you ask mamma to let me go out in the morning with the milkman?

[RICHARD: With the milkman?]

ARCHIE: [Yes.] In the milkcar. He says he will let me drive when we get on the roads where there are no people. The horse is a very good beast. Can I go?

[RICHARD: Yes.]

ARCHIE: Ask mamma now can I go. Will you?

[RICHARD: (*Glances towards the door.*) I will.]

ARCHIE: He said he will show me the cows he has in the field. Do you know how many cows he has?

[RICHARD: How many?]

ARCHIE: Eleven. Eight red and three white. But one is sick now. No, not sick. But it fell.

[RICHARD: Cows?]

ARCHIE: (*With a gesture.*) [Eh! Not bulls. Because bulls give no milk. Eleven cows. They must give a lot of milk.] What makes a cow give milk?

[RICHARD: (*Takes his hand.*) Who knows? Do you understand what it is to give a thing?

ARCHIE: To give? Yes.

RICHARD: While you have a thing it can be taken from you.]

ARCHIE: [By] robbers? No?

[RICHARD: But when you give it, you have given it. No robber can take it from you. (*He bends his head and presses his son's hand against his cheek.*) It is yours then forever when you have given it. It will be yours always. That is to give.]

ARCHIE: But, pappie?

[RICHARD: Yes?]

ARCHIE: How could a robber rob a cow? Everyone would see him. In the night, perhaps.

[RICHARD: In the night, yes.]

ARCHIE: Are there robbers here like in Rome?

[RICHARD: There are poor people everywhere.]

ARCHIE: Have they revolvers?

[RICHARD: No.]

ARCHIE: Knives? Have they knives?

[RICHARD: (*Sternly.*) Yes, yes. Knives and revolvers.]

ARCHIE: (*Disengages himself.*) Ask mamma now. She is coming.

[RICHARD: (*Makes a movement to rise.*) I will.]

ARCHIE: No, sit there, pappie. You wait and ask her when she comes back. I won't be here. I'll be in the garden.

[RICHARD: (*Sinking back again.*) Yes. Go.]

ARCHIE: [(*Kisses him swiftly.*)] Thanks.

(HE *runs out quickly by the door at the back leading into the garden.*)

FRED, FORMERLY

BY DYLAN DAWSON

FRED, *10-12, is a serious yet creative kid with a chip on his shoulder about having to move away from all of his friends.* HE *is all business. At rise,* HE *unfolds a piece of paper.*

SCENE

The living room or family room of a small home somewhere in the Midwest.

TIME

Early August. The "big move" looms large.

FRED: Okay, let's focus in you guys. We focused in? Great.

I know you didn't think I was serious, but guess what, here it is, and in alphabetical order so you aren't influenced by which are my favorites. Don't get me wrong, there IS another list in my back pocket and that list IS in order of my personal favorites, and there IS a strong—VERY strong—number one. But I want your opinion, especially since this is going to apply to you guys more than anybody—more than *me* even, unless I start talking like a, um…which is that? Which person? *Third* person. Right. Unless I start talking third person like Kenny's older brother likes to do—and I won't because Kenny's older brother is a jerk and a half....But yeah, it's important to me that your guys' favorite be taken into consideration.

Okay, so. Mom? Dad? When we move to Arizona, I wish to change my name to one of the following:

1. Adam Adamantium. Possible nicknames for this one are "Wolverine" or "The Claw."
2. Buddy Badapple.
3. Captain. (*Beat.*) That's it, just Captain.
4. Denzel Jefferson.
5. Griff Hartley. Griff is short for Griffin, ps.
6. Six. Or maybe Captain Six, I dunno.
7. Tennessee Williams. I saw that on a book cover and liked the sound of it.
8. Tom Brady. You guys can just say it was a coincidence or something.
9. Xander. With an X.

And 10. Zander, again. But with a Z.

Now. Judging by your expressions I can tell you're having trouble picking just one name off this list—and *believe me*, I know how you feel. I mean, it took me two weeks to narrow it down from the original seventy-eight I had originally! So feel free to take your time with this decision. We still have the rest of the summer before the new and improved name goes into effect. But don't put it off too long—Dad I'm looking at you!—because I mean it! When that moving truck crosses that state line, and this "new chapter" (or whatever you guys keep calling it) begins, Fred's getting left behind. Fred's gonna just hang out here with his old friends and go to his old school and do all the old things Fred likes to do. Don't worry, if and *when* we ever come back here, guess who'll be waiting? That's right.

Ol' Freddy's gonna be—yes I *know* I'm talking in third person, Mom! I don't like it any more than you do! But to quote the both of you: *this is the situation now.*

You have three weeks to decide.

No pressure.

(FRED *tosses down the list on the ground.*)

Griff out.

A GOOD ONE

BY ANNIE WOOD

MIKE, *age 10 to 12, shares his experience with Ashley, the girl* HE *has a crush on.*

SCENE

A school cafeteria.

TIME

Lunch.

MIKE: (HE *eats a Jell-O cup or some other kind of cafeteria food.*) Ashley told me that she liked me just as "a friend." She told me last month during assembly. I mean, Ashley is the most popular girl at Northstop Middle School. She's sweet and pretty and nice to everyone. Which is kind of the problem. I guess I thought that she was being nice to me because she *liked* me, but it turns out she was being nice to me because she is…nice. Which really stinks. I mean, before Ashley I was just Mike Brown, normal kid with normal friends and a normal life. If life was a fairly tale, I wouldn't be a frog, but I wouldn't be the king either. When I was around Ashley, I sure *felt* like a King. But, just yesterday, we were waiting in line together at lunch. Well, not exactly together, but, she was in front of me and I was right behind her…a couple of people may have been in between us.…Anyhow, I told her this lame joke. I had to kind of yell it to her since there were all those people between us. I yelled to her, "Hey, Ashley, what does Geronimo say when he jumps out of a plane!?" She looked at me strangely for a second and then said, "I don't know. What?" "*MEEEEEEE!!!*" Then there was this pause that lasted for probably just a few seconds but felt like forever. And then the most amazing thing happened. She laughed. (HE *imitates her laugh.*) It was such a wonderful sound. (HE *imitates her laugh again.*) I made Ashley Rubin, the most popular, prettiest, coolest girl in school, laugh. And it wasn't just a little giggle, it was a huge laugh. I could tell she meant it. (HE *imitates her laugh one more time.*) This was it! This was my moment! Ashley was going to get her usual one apple, one mashed potato boat, and one chocolate milk and then come over to me and profess her undying love. This is the moment I've been waiting for my entire life! I am so ready. Ashley Rubin walked right up to me, she was so close I could smell the Cherry Vanilla Shampoo in her hair…she looked me straight in the eye and said, "Good one, Mike." Good one, Mike. (MIKE *is a bit let down but recovers.*) Well, even if it was just for a second…it was good to be king.

THE HANDICAPPERS

BY BOB SHUMAN

ROLAND, *11 years old, gives eyewitness testimony after being chased by the mob—as well as the police—for attempting to divert attention from himself and his mother's boyfriend, a short-order cook named Louie.* (NOTE TO ACTOR: THE MONOLOGUE CAN BE DONE WITH, OR WITHOUT, A YO-YO.)

SCENE
Toward the parking lot of Monmouth Park Race Track in New Jersey.

TIME
Spring.

ROLAND: Well. I get up at five-thirty in the morning, so I have Cocoa Puffs and orange Tang. We're takin' a subway ride to Jersey Transit at Penn Station: Get off at Forty-second Street, not Thirty-fourth—'cause Louie—he's over here—wants to meet the Princess—she's over there—at the track for a job. I'm fallin' asleep on the Racin' Form, looking out the dirty windows, the number four reiteratin' in my head concernin' the third race at Monmouth Park.

(ROLAND *takes a yo-yo from his pocket and, tentatively, begins using it.*)

Ma could live happily ever after with Louie—and all I'd have to do is move *out*. Then the driver has to pull over cause I gotta go to the baffroom.

(ROLAND *does a Tidal Wave with his yo-yo; as* HE *continues the monologue, his tricks become more involved.*)

I shoulda taken a departure schedule at the gate but I like lookin' at all the waterways. I want to feed a wounded horse, like a docta. I'm imaginin' what would happen wakin' up every morning in a place that smells like a flowa garden. When we unload, Louie starts teachin' me how to climb the big fence...but I guess I don't need to tell you how they break in. (*Changing the subject.*)

(ROLAND *does a Breakaway, for example:* HE *continues to yo-yo, adding loops as* HE *goes.*)

(*Referring to the Conductor.*) *This* guy over here says, "Our humanity is departing us," and I wonder what happens to those people who don't lose it, who can't lose it for no apparent reason. Then—it's like some kind of dream except it can't be—everything starts goin' from bad to worse...to worser still...like a nightmare. The Conductor turns into a hitman and the Princess belongs to the mob; the violin becomes a gun and the horse, horse number four, loses....All of a sudden, I realize, I figure out, life is short, I ain't gonna be livin' no more, I need to run, and I gotta grab a pair of angel's wings. The violin, in the case, isn't a gun, it isn't even the doe-re-mi. It's...laundry. I hear it then—from outta nowhere—somebody starts talkin': "Take care of Louie." Listen to this! Not like some voice from God. Like a punk, like some twerp! In this high voice: "Take care of Louie!" That's what it starts sayin! Ain't no angels. I don't know what it is. I look around, all I see is...just these mugs goin' to jail. (*Considering.*) "Take care of Louie": He can't hear. I can't pass math. The laundry is dirty.

I don't know how much or who is out there, I don't know where that voice came from: All I know is we got left. *We* get left. We're the undeparted.

HENRY V
BY WILLIAM SHAKESPEARE

The BOY *is English, early to mid-teens, and has come to France serving corrupt soldiers—Bardolf, Nym, and Pistol—*HE *dislikes and hopes to get away from. In the past, the* BOY *served as a page to Falstaff, an earthy knight and king's tutor who has died.*

SCENE
Before Harfleur, a French port.

TIME
1415 A.D.

BOY: As young as I am, I have observed these three swashers. I am boy to them all three: but all they three, though they would serve me, could not be man to me; for indeed three such antics do not amount to a man. For Bardolph, he is white-livered and red-faced; by the means whereof a' faces it out, but fights not. For Pistol, he hath a killing tongue and a quiet sword; by the means whereof a' breaks words, and keeps whole weapons. For Nym, he hath heard that men of few words are the best men; and therefore he scorns to say his prayers, lest a' should be thought a coward: but his few bad words are matched with as few good deeds; for a' never

broke any man's head but his own, and that was
against a post when he was drunk. They will steal
any thing, and call it purchase. Bardolph stole a
lute-case, bore it twelve leagues, and sold it for
three half pence. Nym and Bardolph are sworn
brothers in filching, and in Calais they stole a
fire-shovel: I knew by that piece of service the
men would carry coals. They would have me as
familiar with men's pockets as their gloves or their
handkerchers: which makes much against my manhood,
if I should take from another's pocket to put into
mine; for it is plain pocketing up of wrongs. I
must leave them, and seek some better service:
their villainy goes against my weak stomach, and
therefore I must cast it up.

"JABBERWOCKY" FROM THROUGH THE LOOKING-GLASS

BY LEWIS CARROLL

A NARRATOR, *any age, tells of the slaying of a legendary creature.*

SCENE

A dream.

TIME

'Twas brillig (4:00 in the afternoon).

NARRATOR: 'Twas brillig, and the slithy toves
Did gyre and gimble in the wabe;
All mimsy were the borogoves,
And the mome raths outgrabe.

"Beware the Jabberwock, my son!
The jaws that bite, the claws that catch!
Beware the Jubjub bird, and shun
The frumious Bandersnatch!"

He took his vorpal sword in hand:
Long time the manxome foe he sought—
So rested he by the Tumtum tree,
And stood awhile in thought.

And as in uffish thought he stood,
The Jabberwock, with eyes of flame,
Came whiffling through the tulgey wood,
And burbled as it came!

One, two! One, two! And through and through
The vorpal blade went snicker-snack!
He left it dead, and with its head
He went galumphing back.

"And hast thou slain the Jabberwock?
Come to my arms, my beamish boy!
O frabjous day! Callooh! Callay!"
He chortled in his joy.

'Twas brillig, and the slithy toves
Did gyre and gimble in the wabe;
All mimsy were the borogoves,
And the mome raths outgrabe.

JAKE'S SPEECH

BY B. J. BURTON

JAKE ADAMS, *a boy between 10 and 12 years old, stands in the front of his middle school class, next to his teacher, Mrs. Parker.* HE*'s not happy about speaking in front of them.* HE*'s even less happy about being the first in the class to do so.*

SCENE

A middle school classroom.

TIME

The present.

JAKE: Hey....Hello....Good morning, Mrs. Parker. Good morning, class people. (HE *takes a deep breath.*) Our assignment is to tell you—, is to do an oral presentation, on the most traumatic event in our lives....Geez, are you kidding me? You want us to talk about this?...Sorry for the outburst, but I mean, really, it's one thing to ask us to write about it, but to talk about it in public... and, you're making me go first again? Really Mrs. Parker, is that fair? I'm thinking of changing my name from Adams to Zadams, so I don't have to go first all the time. And I'm sure my story isn't anything compared to most, ya know? (*A beat.*) So when I was eight, I fell off my skateboard and hit a pole with a rusty nail sticking out of it. There was a gash in my leg that wouldn't stop bleeding. I didn't want to tell my mom because she'd just yell or tell me it was my stupid fault. So, it bled all night, soaked through the sheets. I woke up to my mom screaming over my head. I thought someone was dying, but it was me. I threw up what there was to throw up, then I fell on the floor. I don't remember anything 'cept Oxford, that's my dog. He's an English bulldog, we think. He looked at me and he threw up, too. When I woke up in the hospital, my mom was there, her mascara streaming down her cheeks, splotching up her pink uniform. I survived, ya know?...Oh, yeah, I got a tetanus shot, too, because if I didn't, I'd foam at the mouth and bite all my teachers! Just kidding, Mrs. P....Oh, you want more? I can show you the scar on my leg. Wanna see?...No? Maybe later.

The thing was, I almost died. They told me that. "We almost lost you, son." That's what they said, the doctors and all. It was totally cool that I didn't expire, ya know?...So, I know you want us to say what we got out of this experience, like if it taught us anything. Well, like I said, I got this scar! That's what I got out of it!...I'm not being flip, Mrs. P. That's what you asked, right?... Okay, okay. Gimme a sec. Yeah, so now I maybe know for sure that my mom cares. She missed a lot of work to take care of me. So, yeah, now I know that for sure, and that's not a small thing. Sincerely, Jake Zadams.

JASON

BY SANDRA CROFT

While befriending a new boy in his class, JASON, *11-14, riffs on the lame ways that kids try to flatter their teachers.*

SCENE

The school playground.

TIME

Recess.

JASON: If you're going to be a brown-noser, at least do it right. And with Mrs. Post, you gotta get creative 'cause she's grumpy. She doesn't like kids. I mean, if you're going to be a teacher, shouldn't you actually *like* kids? All last week, I counted the times Mrs. Post smiled. Two. And those were when the lunch bell rang. And she yells a lot. "QUIET DOWN, CLASS! THIS ISN'T A ZOO!" I've got shell shock and I'm only— (*Actor, insert your age.*) Anyway, take Kevin Connor, for example. Mrs. Post comes into class and he says, "You look beautiful today." Beautiful? Mrs. Post has hair resembling a Brillo pad helmet—and a mustache. A smarter brown-noser would say, "Mrs. Post, I like your sweater," which would at least be true, 'cause she seems to put all her money into button-down sweaters. She's always buying new ones—I think 'cause she has the shoulders of an NFL linebacker, if you know what I mean. And then there's Emily. Whenever she gets her test back, she says, "I liked that test." What kind of idiot likes tests? It's like saying, "Thank you; I really needed a little torture in my life." Or how about Frankie? Every time we have a bake sale, his mom makes cupcakes. And every time, he comes in and says, "Mrs. Post, would you like a cupcake? Free, of course." Like Mrs. Post really needs a cupcake. A coupon for Nutrisystem would be a better idea. Or a happy pill—if they could put cheerfulness into a pill. Yeah, Mrs. Post could use a giant bottle of happy pills—chocolate-coated. Know what I mean? See, I've got this system all figured out. Just stick with me and you'll be golden. Say, did you do today's homework? Yeah? How'd you like to do a big favor for your new best friend?

KING JOHN

BY WILLIAM SHAKESPEARE

Because of a rival claim to the English throne, King John wants his nephew, ARTHUR, *8-12, Duke of Brittany, to be blinded and killed. Although* ARTHUR *will ultimately fall to his death trying to escape, here,* HE *is able to convince his guard, Hubert de Burgh, to spare his life.*

SCENE

England. A castle.

TIME

1203 A.D.

ARTHUR: Have you the heart? When your head did but ache,
I knit my handercher about your brows,
The best I had, a princess wrought it me,

And I did never ask it you again;
And with my hand at midnight held your head,
And like the watchful minutes to the hour,
Still and anon cheer'd up the heavy time,
Saying, "What lack you?" and "Where lies your grief?"

Or "What good love may I perform for you?"
Many a poor man's son would have lien still

And ne'er have spoke a loving word to you;
But you at your sick service had a prince.
Nay, you may think my love was crafty love
And call it cunning: do, an if you will:
If heaven be pleased that you must use me ill,
Why then you must. Will you put out mine eyes?
These eyes that never did nor never shall
So much as frown on you.

THE LOMAN FAMILY PICNIC

BY DONALD MARGULIES

Realizing the parallels between his own life, Arthur Miller's, and the play DEATH OF A SALESMAN, MITCHELL, *11, decides to write a musical.* HE *talks directly to the audience in this play, which moves between fantasy and reality.*

SCENE
Coney Island, Brooklyn, New York.

TIME
1965.

MITCHELL: For school, Miss Schoenberg made us read this play that Arthur Miller wrote a long time ago, before I was born, about this salesman with two sons who lives in Brooklyn? Sound familiar? I know; I read it like three times 'cause I couldn't believe it either. There are all these similarities. Except Willy Loman, the guy in the play?, the salesman?, doesn't sell lighting fixtures. (*Beat.*) Anyway, in the play he goes insane and kills himself by smashing up his car so his family can collect his insurance money, even though I thought you can't collect if you commit suicide, which is what I said in class but Miss Schoenberg said not necessarily. (*Beat.*) Arthur Miller himself grew up in this very same spot practically. Many years ago. He walked the same streets I walk every day. He played in our schoolyard probably. I heard that his family's house was one of the houses they wrecked so they could build our middle-income luxury building here in Coney Island. At least that's what Miss Schoenberg said. (*Beat.*) Anyway, we have to get up in front of the class and do like oral book reports? But instead of doing the usual if-you-want-to-know-how-he-kills-himself-you-have-to-read-the-play-kind of thing, I decided I'm gonna do something else, something different. (*Beat.*) So, I'm writing this musical-comedy version of *Death of a Salesman* called *Willy!* With an exclamation point. You know, like *Fiorello!*? *Oklahoma! Oliver!*? So far I've come up with a couple of songs. Like, when Biff and Happy are up in their room and they hear Willy downstairs talking to himself? They sing this song called "Dad's a Little Weird" which goes: (*Sings.*) "Dad's a little weird, he's in a daze. Could it be he's going nuts, or is it just a phase?? (*Beat.*) Well, it's a start. What do you think?

THE LOMAN FAMILY PICNIC

BY DONALD MARGULIES

MITCHELL, *11, continues to work on his musical version of* DEATH OF A SALESMAN, *conceptualizing a number where his family goes on a picnic to Prospect Park in Brooklyn.* HE *talks directly to the audience.*

SCENE
Coney Island, Brooklyn, New York.

TIME
1965.

MITCHELL: There's this scene in my musical that's not in the original. All the Lomans go off on a picnic together to Prospect Park. I thought it would lighten things up a little bit. *You* know, a little up-tempo production number. (*Beat.*) Everybody's young and happy. Biff's wearing his varsity T-shirt and he and Happy are tossing around the football, and Linda's setting the picnic table with laminated paper plates and potato salad and coleslaw, and Willy's at the barbecue in a Kiss-the-Cook apron, flipping the franks. He's got the day off for a change, and he sings something like "Oh What a Beautiful Morning," only that's already been done, but you know what I mean. "What a Picnic!" Something like that. And Willy's dead brother Ben is there, and Charley and Bernard from next door. Even the woman from Boston is there, disguised as a park attendant and laughing all the time. (*Beat.*) They're all happy. Everybody. And it's very sunny, but not too hot, and there's no wind blowing away the napkins, and no bees or ants, I mean the insect kind, 'cause there are aunts and uncles and cousins and grandparents....It's a perfect day—maybe that's it: (*Sings.*) "What a perfect day for a picnic!" Yeah, and the whole family sings in harmony, really beautiful, like on the *Sound of Music* record when they sing "How do you solve a problem like Maria?" (*Beat.*) You know, this picnic idea I really like. I love picnics. (*Beat.*) We never go on any picnics.

MACBETH

BY WILLIAM SHAKESPEARE

In order to foresee Macbeth's future (he has become king of Scotland through murder and will, ultimately, be killed by Macduff), 3 witches conjure 3 APPARITIONS*—2 of which are kids! Here, we've grouped all the warnings together (that of an armed head, a bloody child, and a child crowned, with a tree in his hand).*

SCENE

A cave. In the middle, a cauldron boiling. Thunder.

TIME

Morning.

FIRST APPARITION: Macbeth! Macbeth! Macbeth! beware Macduff;
Beware the thane of Fife. Dismiss me. Enough.

(*Descends.*)

(*Thunder.* SECOND APPARITION: *A bloody Child.*)

SECOND APPARITION: Macbeth! Macbeth! Macbeth!
Be bloody, bold, and resolute; laugh to scorn
The power of man, for none of woman born
Shall harm Macbeth.

(*Thunder.* THIRD APPARITION: *a Child crowned, with a tree in his hand.*)

THIRD APPARITION: Be lion-mettled, proud; and take no care
Who chafes, who frets, or where conspirers are:
Macbeth shall never vanquish'd be until
Great Birnam wood to high Dunsinane hill
Shall come against him.

(*Descends.*)

MARICELA DE LA LUZ LIGHTS THE WORLD

BY JOSÉ RIVERA

On their journey, Maricela and her brother Riccardo enter a volcano and meet a melancholy CYCLOPS *(11-14). Here,* HE *tells his story.*

SCENE
Los Angeles.

TIME
Now.

CYCLOPS: Why? Why am I here? Why was I ever born? Oh, unhappy me! Ugly, lonely, living in this sulphurous pit, surrounded by emptiness, cold, discarded, demeaned, depressed! Why? Why should there be a creature whose only reason for being is to provide the world with a supreme example of abject misery? And why should that creature be me? Why? If there is only one me in the world—only one—why does that me have to be me?! And worst of all—I can't see a thing anymore! My one eye is suited only for the dark. For the deep caverns and rococo labyrinths of the volcano, where there is no green, no life, no sunshine, nothing to see but the hard numbing monotony of granite. Above the ground, where there should be life in abundance—dear, deaf stars, my only audience!—snow covers everything: and the snow is too bright for my one massive pupil and I am blinded by the glare! Oh, I am truly a wretched creature!

MATTHEW AND STEPHEN

BY JEAN-ROCK GAUDREAULT

STEPHEN, *10-12, comes charging out of his house, visibly furious. We hear his mother calling him.* HE *has just moved to a new town and misses his old school, where* HE *was captain of the dodgeball team.* HE *hasn't made any new friends yet.*

SCENE

In front of STEPHEN*'s house, which is blue.*

TIME

Before the start of the school year.

STEPHEN: No, I won't go to that school! I didn't want to move, nobody asked my opinion! I don't know anyone around here!... Make new friends? It's too hard, it takes too long. (HE *looks around.*) No mountains, no woods...just houses that all look the same. And papers on the ground everywhere. It doesn't smell of flowers, it smells of cars....The sky is different, it's so low, looks like it's going to hit the chimneys. There's nowhere to pick raspberries, you have to buy them at the store. And besides, my room is smaller, much smaller. It smells of paint. We didn't take a vacation because of the move...I don't like it here. I don't want to grow up here. I want everything to be like it was before!

(STEPHEN *is crying.*)

A MIDSUMMER NIGHT'S DREAM

BY WILLIAM SHAKESPEARE

PUCK, *10 or ageless, is page to the king of the fairies, Oberon.* HE *sends* PUCK *to seek an Athenian couple wandering in the woods.* PUCK *discovers different Athenians sleeping there and, mistakenly, administers his love concoction to the eyes of the male, Lysander.*

SCENE
In a clearing in the woods.

TIME
Timeless.

PUCK: Through the forest have I gone.
But Athenian found I none,
On whose eyes I might approve
This flower's force in stirring love.

Night and silence.—Who is here?
Weeds of Athens he doth wear:
This is he, my master said,
Despised the Athenian maid;
And here the maiden, sleeping sound,
On the dank and dirty ground.
Pretty soul! she durst not lie

Near this lack-love, this kill-courtesy.
Churl, upon thy eyes I throw
All the power this charm doth owe.
When thou wakest, let love forbid
Sleep his seat on thy eyelid:
So awake when I am gone;
For I must now to Oberon.

A MIDSUMMER NIGHT'S DREAM

BY WILLIAM SHAKESPEARE

PUCK, *10 or ageless, leads a group of fairies in blessing the marriages of 2 Athenian couples, Demetrius and Helena and Lysander and Hermia, whose love lives have been confused because of* PUCK*'s well-intentioned mischief.*

SCENE

A wood outside Athens.

TIME

What you will.

PUCK: Now the hungry lion roars,
And the wolf behowls the moon;
Whilst the heavy ploughman snores,
All with weary task fordone.
Now the wasted brands do glow,
Whilst the screech-owl, screeching loud,
Puts the wretch that lies in woe
In remembrance of a shroud.
Now it is the time of night
That the graves all gaping wide,
Every one lets forth his sprite,
In the church-way paths to glide:

And we fairies, that do run
By the triple Hecate's team,
From the presence of the sun,
Following darkness like a dream,
Now are frolic: not a mouse
Shall disturb this hallow'd house:
I am sent with broom before,
To sweep the dust behind the door.

A MIDSUMMER NIGHT'S DREAM

BY WILLIAM SHAKESPEARE

PUCK *addresses the audience after the weddings of 2 Athenian couples confused by an evening in the woods.* HE *explains that if the characters have in any way offended, think of them as part of a dream.*

SCENE
Outside Athens.

TIME
The honeymoon.

PUCK: If we shadows have offended,
Think but this, and all is mended,
That you have but slumber'd here
While these visions did appear.
And this weak and idle theme,
No more yielding but a dream,
Gentles, do not reprehend:
if you pardon, we will mend:
And, as I am an honest Puck,
If we have unearned luck
Now to 'scape the serpent's tongue,
We will make amends ere long;

Else the Puck a liar call;
So, good night unto you all.
Give me your hands, if we be friends,
And Robin shall restore amends.

MY SUPERPOWER

BY LUCY WANG

STAN LEE, *a 12- to 14-year-old Asian-American boy, has learned how to protect himself and his dreams against a tide of expectations and preconceived notions. All* HE *had to do was to find his own superpower.*

SCENE
Anywhere you choose.

TIME
The present.

STAN: When you look like me, people automatically assume that I am a (*Gets into a stance, hands up, right leg up in the air.*) kung-fu master! (HE *kicks an imaginary opponent.*) Hah-ya! Take that, weak earthling. (*Left jab followed by a right cross.*) And that I have superpowers. I can kickbox, karate-chop, and mix-martial-arts you into a zillion pieces—all with my eyes closed. Not. But no one ever believes me. Never. The other boys are always trying to pick fights, challenge me. Pushing and shoving. Breaking into my locker. "Show me what you got, Stan!" I suppose it's only natural. Bruce Lee, Jet Li, (*Refers to himself.*) Stan Lee. Yeah, my parents named me after that Stan Lee. The guy who created Spiderman, the Hulk, and Captain America. What a terrible mistake. What were my parents thinking, giving me a name like that? You can't name a kid Stan Lee and expect to him to succeed on his own, without a mask, without a sword! Yes, a sword. Like this. (HE *wields an imaginary épée and starts thrusting, flexing the wrist, lunging, showing off various techniques throughout the remainder of the monologue.*) It's called an épée. You grip it like a small bird in your hand. But it's no small bird. Oh no. Sharp. Dangerous. Quick. I could cut you if you come too close. Ask me to spin a web. Turn green. Blind you with my shield. And I could, so don't test me.

My parents told me I had three career choices. Doctor. Physician. M.D. To that, I say, Please! Don't fence me in. Don't make me draw blood. I want to be a musician. Rock Star Performer. Write music and play the guitar. For millions and millions of adoring fans worldwide. So please, don't stand in my spotlight. I'm still exploring my powers, so if I were you, I'd keep a proper distance. (*Lunges and thrusts.*) It's for your protection and mine. Of course it's a huge risk, I could go down in flames, but superheroes risk their lives all the time. Usually for damsels in distress, furry pets and crying babies, I know. But don't you think that a superhero has to learn how to save himself before he can save others? (*A beat.*) Hello, I'm Stan Lee, and I'm working on my superpower.

NEW

BY CRYSTAL SKILLMAN

A hot, lead actor, Marcus, *14, hasn't arrived at the theatre, and the show has started;* He *has been AWOL since last night's dress rehearsal and now* He*'s supposed to go on! Suddenly—with a teen playwright and director freaking out—*Marcus, *an overly dramatic thespian still dressed in his Victorian costume from last night, bursts through the door (with a now mysterious bandage on his head), refusing to go on.*

SCENE
Backstage.

TIME
Just before the cue.

Marcus: No! I can't go out there! Last night—I felt it in my bones, in every molecule as you gave us notes, and Ronald patted me on the back. As I came out to the parking lot, past the cool kids—even they knew that I had nailed the dress rehearsal!—congratulating me—I had triumphed. I look up—at the moon—and I know I have to keep walking. Up the block. Past the cars, past the lights, telephone poles, dead raccoons that were once living, breathing as I was, as I am. And there I was—here I am! (He *is now reenacting his night dramatically.*) At the park: Where the scouts would take us when we were kids for drama camp!

Closed. But not for me. Not for Marcus! I jump the fence. Onto the grass. The straw on the ground from the horses, now in the barn—the ones we came out and rode to do research for last year's production of *Equus* and again: the moon! Following me! And in its glow I feel my success of the night: The laughter, the cries of happiness, the notes in the dressing room from the cast and crew, the texts buzzing in my pocket. At the lake: The frogs, the gnats, the green weird stuff on top suffocating the rest, and I look into a patch of it, and I see in my eyes what I knew was there all along—me without fear. Everything I was, old, gone. Me, breathing, living, being—not the mortal Marcus who pretends to have been named after the bard's play. The truth is my mom heard the name on a Hewlett Packard commercial—No! Marcus, who has dreams! Marcus, who is realizing them. Marcus, who knows what being perfect is and feels it in every part of him. Marcus, who is one with everything in the world. The stars! Ready to declare! Ready to tweet my glory—my amazing performance to the world when my iPhone falls…into the deadly murk—the water! It's gone! And I am alone. And, for the first time, I hear the rain—the wind—the air. (HE *imitates.*) And I realize—that was just rehearsal. I have to go on again! And again. But how? How can I achieve that again? I just know how to be Marcus but how can Marcus be better than Marcus? I gasp! The success burning moments before in me slipping away—the me I crave. The future I dream of! (HE *rants about his future.*) A star the minute I graduate! Accepted at Juilliard! In an Adam Rapp play in a black box theatre on St. Marks in the East Village! On TV! *Law and Order*—*CSI*! *Bones*! Insurance commercials. *Big Bang Theory*! Living! My life! At twenty-two on a New York City fire escape. Christmas bulb lights with only one working light. One tuna fish can in the kitchen. My bohemian dreams slipping away because I can't go out there again! I crawl back here—my heart lost—past skateboarder kids on the highway, hobos rummaging through trashcans. Thirsty, stop at a bodega…a fat man lights his cigar and my anger at myself bursts!—"Hey, you ever think of—quitting!" And all I see is his fist coming towards (*Grasps the bandage over his eye, reliving the moment.*) my eye! Like Christopher Marlowe, my eyes are open because I can see! Love. It's a word I can't say. I won't say it. Last night, I could because it was new. That was the secret! Last night, I saw you in the wings and I could only act—pretend to speak words of love. But now! I am! I am Marcus who has been missing for the past twenty hours and who has fought and changed and come home—I am Marcus who has conquered the air, the moon, and I am here. I'm present. I'm new. I love you. I want love. I want one kiss and I can go out there. Can I kiss you? I kiss you! (He *does.*) And I am love! Pull back the curtain! Enter—Marcus! Yes!

THE NORTH WIND AND THE SUN

BY AESOP

A TRAVELER, *7 or any age, wears a winter coat.*

SCENE

Outside.

TIME

Day.

TRAVELER: (*Buttons coat.*) The North Wind and the Sun had a quarrel about which of them was the stronger. While they were arguing with much heat and bluster, a Traveler passed along the road wrapped in a cloak.

"Let us agree," said the Sun, "that he is the stronger who can strip that Traveler of his cloak."

"Very well," growled the North Wind, and at once sent a cold howling blast against the Traveler.

(*Make or play the sound of wind.*)

With the first gust of wind the ends of the cloak whipped about the Traveler's body. But he immediately wrapped it closely around him, and the harder the Wind blew, the tighter he held it to him.

(*The* TRAVELER *does just this.*)

The North Wind tore angrily at the cloak, but all his efforts were in vain.

Then the Sun began to shine. At first his beams were gentle, and in the pleasant warmth after the bitter cold of the North Wind, the Traveler unfastened his cloak and let it hang loosely from his shoulders.

(*The* TRAVELER *does this.*)

The Sun's rays grew warmer and warmer. The man took off his cap and mopped his brow. At last he became so heated that he pulled off his cloak, and, to escape the blazing sunshine, threw himself down in the welcome shade of a tree by the roadside.

(*The* TRAVELER *takes off his coat and sits.*)

Gentleness and kind persuasion win where force and bluster fail.

OFF COMPASS

BY KELLY YOUNGER

Ollie is a 12- to 14-year-old farm boy from Kansas with big dreams. He has an encounter at a festival devoted to that American story of big dreams, The Wizard of Oz, where He finds out some surprising truths.

SCENE

In Kansas.

TIME

The present.

Ollie: 'Bout four years ago, my momma took me south to Liberal, down there for the Oz-tober Fest. Not one of them German beer drinking things, but *The Wizard of Oz.* The guy who wrote it was born down there. Whole town dresses up like *The Wizard of Oz.* You know, all the girls as that dumb Dorothy, and everyone else as the scarecrow, the lion, and the oil can guy. But after a couple of years it started getting bigger and the townsfolk got tired of the same costumes. So they started dressing up like Toto or the mayor of Munchkinville with tulips sticking up out of his toes, and then all the little kids had lollypops and suspenders and hats with propellers. They paint a stupid yellow path right through town and parade up and down it. Even paint the horses green.

Year I went, Momma dressed up as the good witch in a big pink dress carrying a wooden spoon wrapped in tin foil. She put a tail on my butt and stupid wings on my back. I told her a flying monkey had no business hanging out with the good witch of the east, or north, or wherever she was from, but she said it didn't matter, and just whacked me with the spoon. Pretty stupid if you ask me. But I was still glad to be there. That is until I went to Dorothy's house. They have this regular old little house, no different from any other house in Kansas, only this one for sure belonged to Dorothy. So you go there, and all these ugly buck-toothed girls are working there as guides. And, yes, they're all dressed in blue dresses and pigtails and ruby slippers. And they've got the dumb movie playing twenty-four hours a day in the gift shop. So Dorothy #7 is giving us a tour and it turns out that the real Dorothy never even set foot in Kansas, let alone in this house. There was this stupid couple from Liberal went to California about twenty years ago to some insurance convention, and, when someone saw Kansas on their name tag, they asked them if they'd ever been to Dorothy's house. It's called sarcasm. So they come back, pick a random house, and declare it to be the door to Oz. And that Frank L. Baum guy wasn't even born there. He's from New York! What a crock. You should have heard Momma go off on this poor girl. Made her give us our money back. Made her cry. Almost hit her with her tin-spoon wand.

Then as we're following the yellow brick road back to the car and driving off, we run into a Munchkin. I mean a real Munchkin. From the movie. And I mean we really ran into him. Hard. Knocked him over. It's not like they show up in the rearview mirror that easy. He's like ninety years old or something, and looked like a potato with a turkey neck. And then he just starts saying, over and over, in a Munchkin voice, "She's really most sincerely dead! She's really most sincerely dead!" And walked off. We got back in the car and drove straight home. That's what I never understood about that lady. Not Momma, but Dorothy. She's all eager to be clicking her heels and get back to Kansas. Or maybe it was really New York. If I was her, I would've got to Oz and kept going. Television says coming up may be the worst tornado season in a decade. I'm planning on sleeping outside.

PENNY-WISE

BY ARABELLA FIELD

CARL, *7-9, speaks directly to the audience about his plan for helping his family.*

SCENE

Anywhere you choose.

TIME

The present.

CARL: Do you know how much one hundred pennies are? Of course you do! One dollar! Do you know how much a thousand are?! Ten thousand? What about a million? A million pennies is a lot of money! I could do a lot with that—it's $10,000! I could help my mom. We could pay off the bank and the credit cards and we could get our car fixed. I could do a lot. Because one day, you know what I realized about pennies? (HE *looks out, expecting a response.*) It's free money! Absolutely free! It's like nobody knows it but there they are, everywhere you go! On the street. In the train. At the store—and they have that—take a penny/leave a penny dish— I always take one. I don't ever leave one…nobody says nothing. I take it and go. I've been doing that for a long time now. I've got so many pennies stashed…I lost count! (HE *is giddy at the thought, and then, as if sharing an important secret,* HE *continues.*) I got up to three thousand one time, but then I messed up and I had to start over again, so now, you know, it's probably more. (HE *feels around in his pockets.* HE *pulls out some change.*) Don't tell nobody, but you can get them at the airport, too. Free! People just leave foreign monies from a foreign country there. When it's not enough to exchange it to our money, yeah they leave it. See? More free money! I made my mom take me once and we found some. A lot. I've got 'em saved and I'll trade them some time. (HE *carefully puts the money safely back in his pocket and checks to feel it is secure.* HE *is quiet and determined.*) If we can just hang on that long. (HE *seems suddenly older.* HE *starts walking away and then stops.*) Don't let my mom know I told you that last part, okay?

PETER PAN, OR THE BOY WHO WOULD NOT GROW UP

BY J. M. BARRIE

PETER PAN, *Hook, and Tink are alone on the island.* PETER PAN *is on the bed, asleep, no weapon near him; Hook is armed to the teeth, sees* PETER*'s medicine seashell, adds 5 drops of poison from a bottle, and exits. A dot of light flashes past him and darts down the nearest tree, looking for* PETER PAN. *It is Tink.*

SCENE

Never Never Land.

TIME

After Hook and the pirates have claimed victory—although they really haven't won—and captured the Lost Boys and Wendy.

PETER PAN: (*Stirring*). Who is that? [(*Tink has to tell her tale, in one long ungrammatical sentence.*)] The redskins were defeated? Wendy and the boys captured by the pirates! I'll rescue her, I'll rescue her! (HE *leaps first at the dagger, and then at his grindstone, to sharpen it.* [*Tink alights near the shell, and rings out a warning cry.*]) Oh, that is just my medicine. Poisoned? Who could have poisoned it? I promised Wendy to take it, and I will as soon as I have sharpened my dagger. [(*Tink, who sees its red colour… nobly swallows the draught as* PETER*'s hand is reaching for it.*)] Why, Tink, you have drunk my medicine! [(*She flutters strangely* *about the room, answering him now in a very thin tinkle.*)] It was poisoned and you drank it to save my life! Tink, dear Tink, are you dying? (HE *has never called her "dear TINK" before...*[*She alights on his shoulder, gives his chin a loving bite, whispers "You silly ass," and falls on her tiny bed. The boudoir, which is lit by her, flickers ominously.*] HE *is on his knees by the opening.*)

Her light is growing faint, and if it goes out, that means she is dead! Her voice is so low I can scarcely tell what she is saying. She says—she says she thinks she could get well again if children believed in fairies! (HE *rises and throws out his arms* HE *knows not to whom, perhaps to the boys and girls of whom* HE *is not one.*) Do you believe in fairies? Say quick that you believe! If you believe, clap your hands! ([*Many clap, some don't, a few hiss....*] *But Tink is saved.*) Oh, thank you, thank you, thank you! And now to rescue Wendy!

([*Tink is already as merry and impudent as a grig, with not a thought for those who have saved her....*] PETER... *is frightfully happy....* HE *takes wing.*)

A PORTRAIT OF THE ARTIST AS A YOUNG MAN

BY JAMES JOYCE

An Irish childhood—including its story, song, and language—through the memory of STEPHEN DEDALUS.

SCENE
Dublin.

TIME
Circa 1882.

STEPHEN: Once upon a time and a very good time it was there was a moocow coming down along the road and this moocow that was coming down along the road met a nicens little boy named baby tuckoo…

His father told him that story: his father looked at him through a glass: he had a hairy face.

He was baby tuckoo. The moocow came down the road where Betty Byrne lived: she sold lemon platt.

O, the wild rose blossoms
On the little green place.

He sang that song. That was his song.

> O, the green wothe botheth.

When you wet the bed first it is warm then it gets cold. His mother put on the oilsheet. That had the queer smell.

His mother had a nicer smell than his father. She played on the piano the sailor's hornpipe for him to dance. He danced:

> Tralala lala,
> Tralala tralaladdy,
>
> Tralala lala,
> Tralala lala.

Uncle Charles and Dante clapped. They were older than his father and mother but uncle Charles was older than Dante.

Dante had two brushes in her press. The brush with the maroon velvet back was for Michael Davitt and the brush with the green velvet back was for Parnell. Dante gave him a cachou every time he brought her a piece of tissue paper.

The Vances lived in number seven. They had a different father and mother. They were Eileen's father and mother. When they were grown up he was going to marry Eileen. He hid under the table. His mother said:

—O, Stephen will apologize.

Dante said:

—O, if not, the eagles will come and pull out his eyes.—

Pull out his eyes,
Apologize,
Apologize,
Pull out his eyes.
Apologize,
Pull out his eyes,
Pull out his eyes,
Apologize.

THE ROBOT MONOLOGUE

BY TAMMY ROSE

The nice thing about being a robot is that you don't need anyone, so no one can hurt you. Or so it seems to this YOUNG PERSON, *age 7 to 9.*

SCENE

The Robot's bedroom.

TIME

Right now, in human time.

YOUNG PERSON: I am a robot. Robots do not cry. Robots always do exactly what people tell them to do. But sometimes parents say the wrong things and the robot does it anyway. Like "feed dinner to the cat" when there's no cat food around. Because robots don't know that cats don't like pizza. Robots do not care if their parents get a divorce. Robots don't have parents. Robots don't have hearts. Or the ability to make water with our eyes. So we just sit there. Robots don't hear their parents fighting over who has to spend more time with me. Um, I mean, with the robot-kid. Robots just get shut down and put in a closet. And robot parents never fight. Because robots don't have parents. Or did I already say that? Maybe robots are sad not to have parents. But they don't cry about it, because of course they can't cry. The robots would be happy not to have people yelling at them. Or making them eat all their food. Robots don't eat food. They don't ever have to eat anything. Except candy. Robots really like candy. And nothing ruins their appetite. If somebody was yelling at a robot, and said, "Why did you do that, Robot? Why? Why? Why?" Then a robot wouldn't have to answer. A robot could just stand there and not cry. Or maybe use his magic robot powers to turn back time so that plate wouldn't fall on the floor and break. And all the food could still be eaten and not spilled on the carpet with cat hair. And the parents would still be living in the same house and not fighting all the time. The robot powers could go back to a time before fighting, when everyone was happy and nobody cried. Not the kid or the mom or the dad. Back when there was no yelling. And food still tasted good. That's why, when I grow up, I'm gonna be a robot. And never cry.

THE SEE-SAW TREE

BY DAVID WOOD

JAY, *a bird, 11-13, lands on a branch just above a thrush who is singing loudly, and out of tune (making a dreadful noise). Brashly confident, ready to sell to his reluctant neighbors,* JAY *keeps his wares inside his coat and carries a suitcase filled with special cleaning materials.*

SCENE

A branch of an oak tree—the See-Saw Tree.

TIME

Before the animals learn that their home will be cut down.

JAY: What music fills my ears?...Such tone. Such pitch. Such artistry...Jay's the name, madam. Travelling salesbird supreme...I have been on a flight of exploration, madam, spreading my wings far and wide in search of marketable merchandise. Scouring the countryside for new and exciting lines to offer my lucky customers at bargain prices. Now, madam, what delights do you desire? Aha! See my selection, perfect for the use of building nests. (HE *opens his coat. Inside his wares are neatly displayed.*) Dried grasses, corn stalks, quality mosses, horse hair, sheep's wool for extra warmth, polyethylene and paper. Pick your own, mix 'n' match, yours for the modest sum of two acorns. Couldn't be fairer than that.... Do me a favour....Aha! Think ahead, madam. Think of when your eggs hatch. Think of all those hungry little beaks to feed. No problem. (HE *opens the other side of his coat, revealing more merchandise.*) I've got crab apples, juicy slugs, calorie-stuffed caterpillars, mouthwatering worms, specially selected spiders, meaty maggots and crunchy moths.... Take your pick.... No? Your loss, dear lady, not mine. Happy laying...(HE *approaches Squirrel's nest.*) Wakey, wakey! Anyone home? (*Squirrel appears, carrying out trash.*) Morning, Squirrel! Doing the cleaning? Aha! (HE *opens his suitcase, displaying more wares.*) Just what you need! Bark scourer, fungus flusher, mildew stripper, leafmould remover. Tried and tested. Satisfaction guaranteed...I'm only asking one acorn per item. Give a bird a chance!

SILAS
BY STEPHEN FIFE

An 11- to 13-year-old boy, CHRIS, *mulls over a difficult decision that* HE *was forced to make.*

SCENE
Outside CHRIS*'s home.*

TIME
Now.

CHRIS: I had this dog, Silas...when I was ten. He was a red springer spaniel, dumb as a fencepost, but I loved him....I didn't at first, my mom bought him home from the pet store to teach me how to be responsible—you know, cleaning up after your pet, taking good care of him, training him, stuff like that...but he was so goofy and silly...he used to knock me down when I came home from school, just jump all over me, knock the books out of my hands and slobber all over my face....He had this really bad breath, too, I mean really bad, it used to make me wanna throw up, but then after awhile I'd find myself sittin' through some boring class, just lookin' out the window, and the smell of Silas's breath would come into my nostrils, so strong...then I couldn't wait to get home, sometimes I would run all the way.

Silas had this really bad habit of chasing trucks...laundry trucks, milk trucks, garbage trucks, parcel post, Federal Express, the guy delivering flowers, anything that came through our neighborhood when he was playing outside....He chased them all down the block, just barking so loud, running into the street, right into traffic, no matter how many times I punished him afterwards, no matter how many obedience classes I took him to, no matter how much I begged him not to do it. "Please Silas, please don't," I murmured, kissing his long red eyelashes, looking into his brown eyes...but he always did. "He's gonna get run over and it's gonna be on your head," my mom told me. I knew it was true. I had to do something. But what? I lay awake at night, looking up at the ceiling, hoping that some brilliant idea would come to me. But it never did. (*A beat.*)

Finally one day I put the leash on Silas and took him for this really long walk. We walked for miles and miles and miles, until we came to this really beautiful park, a place where I'd never been. All these families were having picnics, children were playing on the swings, laughing...I bent down and hugged Silas, I kissed him on his red eyelashes and looked into his watery brown eyes, then I took off his leash and his collar. I watched him go bounding off, heading right for this young couple who were playing with their blond child on a pink blanket. I waited until the child put his arms around Silas, and the mom and dad started petting him...then I started running away as fast as I could, and I didn't stop until I was home. (*A beat.*) For the next two months, I kept thinking Silas would be there when I got home, that he would find his way back and knock me down, just licking me like crazy all over.... Sometimes I can still smell his breath when I open the door.

SOMETHING UNEXPECTED

BY MICHAEL EDAN

JESS, *a 14-year-old boy, shares his thoughts about being able to hear sounds that other people cannot.*

SCENE

Could be anywhere.

TIME

Could be any time.

JESS: (HE *speaks directly to the audience.*) I was eleven before I knew that I could hear what other people don't hear. I was playing with my dog, Sampson, out in our neighbor's field, close to the woods. It was late spring. I was just hangin', not really doing or thinking anything. I became aware of this sound...kind of like music—but not. It was different...strange, and very faint. At first I wasn't sure I was really hearing it so I got very still—and, sure enough, it was there. I looked around thinking someone was nearby with a radio or something, but there was no one. I had never heard anything like this sound before. What was it? I got this funny sense that I should turn and, as I did, my head seemed to move upwards on its own. Then I noticed, for the first time, that I was standing underneath this large cherry blossom tree in full bloom. The sound became clearer and then—I just KNEW I was hearing the sound of the blossoms. (HE *basks a moment in the memory.*)

It was so beautiful, unlike anything I'd ever heard. I just stood there listening—then it finally faded away. It was so cool. When I told my mom she said, "Don't tell anyone else." I couldn't keep a thing like that to myself! So, I asked the other kids at school, and the teachers, the school guidance counselor—that was a mistake. They didn't know what I was talking about. Most of them looked at me like I was really weird, some of them laughed, called me Tinker Bell. That's when I knew they couldn't hear like I hear. (*A beat.*) Then I started hearing other things. Mostly wonderful sounds, like fireflies at dusk. (*A cloud of disturbance comes over him.*) Lately, I've noticed I can receive the thoughts of other people. Not necessarily in words. It's a vibration, kind of like a radio wave…I can hear its meaning. I also hear voices. Sometimes I hear my heart, and I want to crawl into it because it sounds so…comforting. In my heart I still feel safe. I don't feel safe in the world.

A THOUSAND CLOWNS

BY HERB GARDNER

NICK BURNS, *12, neat, ordered, organized, and precocious, should be at school. Instead,* HE *is coming out of the kitchen to pour his Uncle Murray—a nonconformist, unemployed writer of television shows for children—a cup of coffee.* NICK *has also retrieved for his uncle, who has just gotten up, a pack of cigarettes.*

SCENE

A one-room, second-floor apartment of borrowed furniture in a brownstone on the Lower West Side of Manhattan.

TIME

8:40 A.M.

NICK: It's a holiday. It's Irving R. Feldman's birthday, like you said.

[MURRAY: Irving R. Feldman's birthday is my own personal national holiday. I did not open it up for the public. He is proprietor of perhaps the most distinguished kosher delicatessen in this neighborhood and as such I hold the day of his birth in reverence.]

NICK: You said you weren't going to look for work today because it was Irving R. Feldman's birthday, so I figured I would celebrate, too, a little.

[**Murray:** Don't kid *me*, Nick, you know you're supposed to be in school. I thought you *liked* that damn genius' school—why the hell—]

Nick: Well, I figured I'd better stay home today till you got up. (*Hesitantly.*) There's something I gotta discuss with you. See, because it's this special school for big brains they watch you and take notes and make reports and smile at you a lot. And there's this psychologist who talks to you every week, each kid separately. He's the biggest smiler they got up there.

[**Murray:** Because you got brains they figure you're nuts.]

Nick: Anyway, we had Show and Tell time in Mrs. Zimmerman's class on Monday; and each kid in the class is supposed to tell about some trip he took and show pictures. Well, y'remember when I made you take me with you to the El Bambino Club on Fifty-second?

[**Murray:** Nick.... You showed and you told.]

Nick: Well, it turned out they're very square up at the Revere School. And sometimes in class, when we have our Wednesday Free-Association-Talk Period, I sometimes quote you on different opinions...

[**Murray:** That wasn't a good idea.]

Nick: Well, I didn't know they were such nervous people there. Murray, they're very nervous there. And then there was this composition I wrote in Creative Writing about the advantages of Unemployment Insurance.

[**Murray:** Why did you write about that?]

NICK: It was just on my mind. Then once they got my record out they started to notice what they call "Significant data." Turns out they've been keeping this file on me for a long time, and checking with that Child Welfare place; same place you got those letters from.

[MURRAY: I never answer letters from large organizations.]

NICK: So, Murray...when they come over here, I figure we'd better...

[MURRAY: When they come *over* here?]

NICK: Yeah, this Child Welfare crowd, they want to take a look at our environment here.

[MURRAY: Oh that's charming. Why didn't you tell me about this before, Nick?]

NICK: Well, y'know, the past coupla nights we couldn't get together.

[MURRAY: That was unavoidable. You know when I have a lot of work you stay up at Mrs. Myers.

NICK: (*Pointing at the dresser.*) Murray; your work forgot her gloves last night.

[MURRAY: That's very bright.]

NICK: Anyway, for the Child Welfare crowd, I figure we better set up some kind of story before they get here.

TREASURE ISLAND

BY KEN LUDWIG, BASED ON THE NOVEL
BY ROBERT LOUIS STEVENSON

Confronting the pirate Long John Silver, JIM HAWKINS, *13, part of an English hunt for treasure in the Caribbean, explains his heroism in thwarting mutineers.*

SCENE
The blockhouse, a small fort controlled by pirates, on Treasure Island in the West Indies.

TIME
1774.

JIM: Cowardly?!

[SILVER: I'm afraid so. And I have to confess, I thought it was, too.]

JIM: (*Shaking with anger.*) You thought so?! You?! The man who kidnapped my father?! The man who trapped him on a ship against his will?! The man who put him to death because you didn't dare stand up to Captain Flint?! [(*WHAP!* JIM *slaps Silver across the face as hard as* HE *can.*)] There's for your "cowardly." And there! [(*WHAP!*)] And there! [(*WHAP!*)]

[(*Silver hasn't flinched at any of these blows. When* Jim *is finished, Silver rubs his cheek and stares at* Jim.)

Silver: If I'd had a son like you, Jim, I can only dream o' the things we might a' done together. But I'll tell ya what. You've got a choice, Jim. Join up with us and take your share as a gentleman o' fortune, or say no and you walks out that door as free as a bird. It's up to you.]

Jim: I know what kind of choices you offer. I saw what you did on the ship to Tom Morgan when he said no.

[(*The pirates murmur in astonishment.*)

Hazard: How'd he know that?

Bonny: Who told him…?]

Jim: So let the worst come to the worst, it's little I care. I've seen too many perish since I fell in with you. But there's one thing I'll tell you before I die: You're in a bad way. The ship's lost, the treasure's lost, men lost; your whole business has gone to wreck; and if you want to know who did it–it was I!! I was in the apple barrel and told the captain what I heard! I cut the ship's cable and brought her where you'll never see her again. I killed Mr. Hands and stopped him from saving the ship for you. And I know where the treasure is and you'll never find it, not in a thousand years!

TWO STEPS FROM THE STARS

BY JEAN-ROCK GAUDREAULT

JUNIOR, *11-12, is walking with his head down, staring at his toes, counting his steps out loud.* HE *loves numbers and is excellent at math—although* HE *has recently failed an easy math test, which* HE *can't quite explain.* HE *wears glasses.*

SCENE
In the street, on the way home from school.

TIME
The afternoon.

JUNIOR: Three hundred and thirty-five. Three hundred and thirty-six. Three hundred and thirty-seven. (HE *closes his eyes, stretches out his arm and points to the left.*) That's the house of the wrinkled old lady who's always looking out her window, watching the corner of the street. She's waiting for somebody to visit her. She's always alone. Her eyes make me sad. (HE *swings his arm around and points to the right.*) And that's the yellow house. It's still for sale. Nobody wants it because there are lots of houses for sale that are much prettier. Last year, their dad left home, you can tell because the truck is never in the driveway and the paint is peeling on the garage. (HE *swings his arm again and points straight ahead.*) From here on, there are four hundred steps to my house. Seven telephone poles, two fire hydrants and one sign saying: Caution, children playing.

(JUNIOR *opens his eyes, looks to the left, shyly waves to the old lady in the window. Then* HE *looks to the right and straight ahead.* HE *continues on his way.*)

Three hundred and thirty-eight. Three hundred and thirty-nine.

TWO STEPS FROM THE STARS

BY JEAN-ROCK GAUDREAULT

JUNIOR, *11-12, has run away from home because* HE *has failed a math test—his friend Margaret has come with him.* HE *is planning on going to Houston to become an astronaut—*HE *also tells Margaret how much she means to him.*

SCENE
Waiting for a train.

TIME
At night.

JUNIOR: Today has been a strange day. Nothing happened the way I planned. You're asleep, Maggie. Maybe if I keep talking, I can guide your dreams....Dream that the two of us are alone in the world, that all the others, the millions and millions of others have left for another planet. We live in a different house every day. We begin every meal with dessert. We change towns when it starts to rain. We learn to drive a car in the deserted streets. We take a plane to travel back to morning, so we can go to bed as late as possible. We make satellites fall out of the sky so we can count the shooting stars. Half of the countries in the world will be mine, the other half, yours. We'll take turns choosing them on a map, one by one. You will take Spain so you can have a castle on a mountaintop. I will take Russia so I can become a spy.... It's our planet, all ours.... Margaret, I know that you exist.

THE UNDERPRIVILEGED CLUB

BY CAROL S. LASHOF

CARLOS *is a middle school student, 12-13 years old, carrying a backpack and his violin, on the way to orchestra practice.*

SCENE

The hallway of a middle school during passing period. The usual chaos: bells ringing, lockers slamming, cell phones emitting various ring tones, students talking, teachers shouting.

TIME

The present.

CARLOS: Hey, my name is Carlos. And I'm starting a club, an after-school club. Maybe you wanna be in it?

I played in a benefit concert last Sunday. Forty-five dollars a ticket. It had a cute name: "Booze and Beethoven." "Strawberries and Strauss." "Chow Down with Chopin." Something like that. That's when I figured out we need a new club at this school. I'm gonna call it "The Underprivileged Club."

You see, the girl who's first violin, first chair, in the school orchestra—Patricia—she's been taking private lessons since she was three. And it shows. She's really good. I play second violin, third chair. And I'm not too bad. Getting better. Patricia's dad organized the concert, and he was the MC. His sister or cousin or something is in this awesome string quartet. They agreed to play, along with some alumni from the school who are kind of famous, too. After everyone played—we sounded totally amazing, by the way—Patricia's dad thanked the audience for coming. For helping out the "underprivileged" students in the orchestra so the orchestra won't be "held back" by kids who can't afford private lessons. Kids like me.

Our school has one of the best youth orchestras in the country. Seriously. We win all kinds of prizes. I really lucked out, getting into school here, my mom says. And it's true. It's also true she can't pay for private lessons for me. No way. And I want those lessons. I need those lessons. Do you know that Vaughan Williams piece—"The Lark Ascending"? You'd remember it if you'd heard it. You know how sometimes when you're listening to music, your mind wanders to other things. But not this piece. It just grabs hold of you. The violin is the lark, and the soloist has this virtuoso passage at the end—it's all trilling and swooping—and the final note is almost impossible to control—it's so out-of-this-world high and so very, very quiet, fading to pure silence as the lark melts into the distant blue and disappears from sight.

I'm trying to learn it. But it's super hard, the hardest thing I've ever tried to play. So yeah, I'll be totally grateful for those private lessons. I'm grateful for the benefit concert. Really. But the thing is, until Sunday, I didn't get it. Where I fit. Now I do. So I'm gonna start a club for all the underprivileged students of the Eastmont Arts and Science Magnet School. We have every other kind of club at our school. The Chess Club. The Ultimate Club. The Ecology Club. The Books Not Bombs Club. Even The Barbecue Club. So why not The Underprivileged Club?

A club for people like me.

UNEXPECTED TENDERNESS

BY ISRAEL HOROVITZ

Roddy, *12-14, talks about the odd quirk that ruled his father's life—his fear of "visitors." He was sure they would invade the family home as soon as the father had left.*

SCENE

The family home, Gloucester, Massachusetts.

TIME

The 1950s.

Roddy: My father never left for work easily. He was always certain that what he called "visitors" would be sneaking into our house, as soon as he was gone. Because he drove his own truck, he was able to drive by the house several times a day and pop in. . . just to check on things. We never knew exactly what kind of "visitors" he expected to find in our house. . .earthlings or aliens. Only he knew for sure. And we never knew exactly what purpose the visitors would have in our particular house. What we did know, however, was not to be frightened when a man almost always appeared, peeking in through one of the ground floor windows, shortly after our father left for work. . .or, shortly before our father got home from work. The fact is, it was kind of a shock the first time I had a sleep-over at Sal Cataldo's house, and his father, Mr. Cataldo, went straight to work and never once showed up in any of the downstairs windows.

YEMAYA'S BELLY

BY QUIARA ALEGRÍA HUDES

Before HE *goes to school,* JESUS (HAY-SOOS), *12, takes a cup of coffee to his father.*

SCENE

At his family's farm in an island town, only accessible by one narrow, winding road.

TIME

Sunrise. Wind blows furiously.

JESUS: Red white and blue
Sugar and gin
My story begins

Once there was a boy. It was Sunday and church was over. The boy wanted to buy a cookie so he asked his papi for a penny. "Oh, papi..." But before the boy could finish his papi yelled, "No!" The boy said, "But papi..." And the papi yelled, "No!" So the boy turned away and whispered, "Stiiingy." Repeat it louder, so I can hear," the papi said. So the boy repeated it. "Stiiiiingy." And then the boy heard a growl come from inside the papi's belly. It sounded like the beginning of a hurricane. The boy took off running so the papi wouldn't smack him with the belt. He ran all the way to the top of the coconut tree. And he spent the night up there and he didn't come down for dinner, even though his mami had made pork chops. That night, the wind was so strong that he flew away. (HE *spreads his arms to fly. The coffee spills to the ground.*) He flew over the farm. He flew over the mountain. He flew over the ocean. He flew all the way to America, and he landed in the house of the President of America. He told the story about his stingy papi, and the President of America gave the boy a penny to buy a sugar cookie.

Red white and blue
Sugar and rum
My story is done

YEMAYA'S BELLY

BY QUIARA ALEGRÍA HUDES

JESUS (HAY-SOOS), *12, sits beside his mami, massaging her skin.*

SCENE

Cuba. A dark place. Mami lies on the ground, still.

TIME

After the fire, which has destroyed JESUS*'s home.*

JESUS: I got some oil to rub your skin. Does it still burn here? (HE *gently massages her side.*) Yesterday you made noises when I touched you here. Why don't you make some noises now? (HE *pokes at her side, seeing if she'll make a noise.*) It's aloe and some other kind of stuff. Special stuff for the burns. Doña Aye made it for you. You put it on the skin, then you move your fingertips in little circles. Like you used to when I was sick. You would rub that tingly stuff on my chest. You would move your fingertips in little circles. It stunk, and then I would fall asleep and dream like I was flying over the mountains.

Can you hear me?

Are you still dreaming about ghosts?

Do you just dream at night or are you dreaming all the time now?

You should eat. (HE *tries feeding her. There's no response.*) I'll sing you a song. How about the one we used to sing on the farm and try to bother papi while he worked. When he was grumpy. (HE *sings a lullaby.*)

I'm going to the sea
To meet my secret love
If she remembers me
The sun
The sun
The sun

([*At the tune, Mami rises from the floor. She sings along.*] *They have a little dance they do when they sing this song.*)

[**MAMI**: I'll sing her all my songs
And as the words are sung
They'll dance within her waves
The sun
The sun
The sun]

JESUS [and **MAMI**]: The sun lives at the edge of the sea
The sun said she would wait there for me
The sun…

[MAMI: I'm going to the sea
To argue with the rain
And when the clouds are gone
The sun
The sun
The sun

(*Mami twirls offstage.*)]

JESUS: Mami? (HE *looks at the spot where she had been lying on the ground.*) I think you're dreaming all the time.

PART THREE

MONOLOGUES BY STUDENTS

The following monologues were all written during the 2009–2010 school year by middle school students in the Los Angeles public school system, working with theatre artists from Center Theatre Group. The students were all 12 years old when they wrote these. Thanks to Traci Cho of CTG for making them available to us.

THE BURNS

BY NATHAN SURKES

It takes a tough girl to be an investigative cop during these tough times. But they don't come much tougher than JESSICA PARKER.

SCENE

At a house on a road called 51st Oak Avenue.

TIME

This explosive moment.

JESSICA PARKER: I heard a boom and saw the light. When I awoke... the house was burning. It was like a giant Christmas tree with a million lights. We were at 51st Oak Avenue. Everywhere I looked, all I saw was light. I felt the surging heat whip across my face like bullets of flame. I heard the loud sirens of police cars and fire trucks, rushing to help. Out of the distance, right next to the house that just exploded, I saw a kid. No, it was a baby! He was just lying there, not moving. I staggered up to help him, hurting with every step. But when I walked up to him, I could see he was gone. I tried not to cry, but the tears leaked out like a dripping faucet. I was feeling so bad, I wanted to die. My name is Jessica Parker, and I work as an investigative cop. I saw a house that was blown up and three people died. It's very sad. Nobody knows why or who did this, but I'm gonna find out. And a minivan in the front driveway had its windshield broken by a flying branch. Man! It makes me depressed to see things like that. None of the neighbors were harmed, but they were very startled from the explosion. If something goes wrong, then I'll find out why. That's my job, and there's nobody better. Nobody. (*Pause.*) But I still feel really bad about that baby. That little tiny baby. Why do things like that have to happen?

THE HAMSTER

BY SARAH ROTH

SARAH *wants a pet hamster, but her mom says "No."* SARAH *knows that obstacles are there to be overcome.*

SCENE
At a pet store.

TIME
Love at first sight.

SARAH: Mom, look at how cute that one is! Can I hold her, please? I know, I know, I can't get her; I just want to hold her. Yes, people *are* allowed to hold them. I saw a lady do it just a few minutes ago. Okay, fine, I'll go ask myself, if I can ever find a person that works here.... Um, excuse me? Can I hold one of those hamsters? I kind of like that tan one over there. Okay, thank you.... Hey Mom, *see?* I told you that I could hold one; she just had to go get the key. Oh, look! Here she comes now! So...um...what should I do? Do I just hold out my hands? Oh, okay, here goes nothing. Mom, she's so soft. Come on, feel her. See? I told you— I have to put her back already? I mean it's only been, like, thirty seconds! Wait! What's she doing? Ewwww! Mom, Mom, *Mom!!!* She went to the bathroom in my hand! No, no, I'm fine. Wait! What? I know I need to wash my hands, but do...do you think I could get her? Just this once?...I *know* we have a dog and a cat at home, but this is different! I promise I would pay for everything that she needs and take care of her! Please, please, please can I get her, Mom? Yes, I still want her even after she— well, you know, after she did what she did. I mean, that's what hamsters do, right? And if you love them enough, then who cares?

I AM JULIANNE FRANK

BY ANNABEL RENSHAW

JULIANNE FRANK *is Anne Frank's younger cousin.* SHE *sits behind a desk, staring off into the distance as if in contemplation. When* SHE *begins to speak,* SHE *is clearly talking to Anne's diary.* (NOTE: JULIANNE FRANK IS A FICTIONAL CHARACTER, MADE UP BY THE AUTHOR.)

SETTING
Anne Frank's bedroom.

TIME
After World War II.

JULIANNE: (SHE *holds a diary.*) Recognize me? Probably not. You might be mistaking me for my cousin Anne. But I am Julianne Frank. Writing in Anne's journal makes me feel a little bit awkward. I'm not sure if it's right. But it could also be a way to release my feelings, to open up my heart a little. Sometimes I feel so alone without my older cousin, at other times I just want to break something. Anne's death has really changed our family a lot. Our mother is working harder at home and Father never gets home earlier than eight o'clock. Each day it gets harder and harder to get out of bed, but isn't everything supposed to get easier with time? Does this heartache mean I am weak or does it mean I really love her? This thought keeps popping into my head—will life ever get normal again? Will Mom ever stop grieving? Will Dad ever not hide his feelings? (JULIANNE *pauses for a moment, then goes to sit on the bed.* SHE *starts to cry into her pillow.* SHE *comes up, her eyes bloodshot and her cheeks tear-stained.*) What happens if I get so sad that I start crying in class and can't stop? Or worse, what if I get so sad that I cry in the house with all my friends while we are saying our Jewish prayers?

I smile sometimes, but most of the time I am just wearing a mask, it's been painted on and as long as I have company, it won't go away. I'll break down someday, but not today. No, not today, it can't be today, things are supposed to get better, and if I cry it will only get worse. I have to go on with my life, don't I? I mean I can't always think about Anne. I keep looking back and it hurts, it hurts that one day we were laughing and playing and singing, and then the next day she was gone. I wish Anne had never told me to write in her journal after she was gone, it's too hard. This was always Anne's way of expressing herself, not mine, and it doesn't feel right.... (SHE *throws the diary on the ground and sits on the floor.* SHE *takes a deep breath.* SHE *looks up at the sky.*)

Am I going crazy? Am I going to be like everyone else in Germany? Crazy, like that homeless man in the town square? Sad and alone. I guess there's no point in being sad because it's over now, every day I'm getting older. But that's also bringing me closer to you, Anne, closer and closer, I will be happy then, dancing and playing with you. I hope you'll be happy to see me, Anne. We'll laugh together and dance. We'll say all the things we never had a chance to before. (SHE *looks down at the diary and smiles.*) This diary is for both of us, Anne! I love you like a sister. (JULIANNE *opens the diary and writes in it.*)

IN THE RAGS OF A HENCHMAN

BY ASHLEY HERNANDEZ

TARASIUN *wanted to be a superhero, a force for good in the world, but instead* HE *has ended up as a henchman for an evildoer. His clothes are rags, and are kept together by pins. His hair is oily, and it is scruffy-looking. A deep sigh is heard. A mouse scurries across the stage. Spotlight on where* TARASIUN *sits;* HE *picks up the mouse and speaks to it gently.*

SCENE

A basement room/prison; it's old and dirty. It used to be a beautiful salon room in one of the nicest homes in the neighborhood. The peach-colored walls are now all moldy and peeling away. The room is almost vacant except for an old wooden chair and a blanket. There are no windows, no heater, and no way out—only a basement door that is obviously locked to keep the prisoner in and the front door. The pipes have gotten all rusty and leak noisily. The traffic in the area is horrible. There are cars honking, drivers swearing, people yelling, and adding to the noise: dogs barking, cats meowing, and babies passing by crying. To make the basement even more unbearable, the moment you step in, you are attacked by the smell of rotten milk, burnt toast, and mouse droppings.

TIME

The present, seemingly unchanging.

TARASIUN: Got you! Hey, little mouse, are you all alone, too? Just like I am. I don't even know how it got this way. All I ever wanted was to be a superhero, somebody like Batman. (HE *sighs.*) I wanted to be my own superhero, somebody loved and cared for, but I ended up here, waiting in darkness until my master needs me. Yes, I am a henchman. I sleep on the cold floors of basements with no heater, only my blanket to keep me warm. I get no reward if I do something right, but I get hurt if I do something wrong. Maybe one day I will finally have the strength to rise up against the evil person I work for and become the superhero that I still have inside me. Oh, the beautiful word "maybe." The one that lets you think of all the wonderful things you can be and how you could reach heaven someday. (HE *looks at the mouse.*) What did you say to me, mouse? "All it takes to be a good person is to start doing good things"? You think it's that easy? Maybe for you, little mouse, but for me…? (*A beat.*) But maybe you're right. Maybe the hardest step to take is the first one. Okay then, here is the first good thing I'm going to do….(HE *lets the mouse go.*) Go! Go, little mouse! Run to freedom! Run, run, keep running! (HE *laughs—something* HE *hasn't done in a long time.*) Yes, you're right! I feel better already! I feel stronger! I love you, little mouse, you have given me hope! (HE *stands.*) I will do it, I will defeat my evil master! I will be a force for good in the world! And it's all thanks to you, little mouse! It's all thanks to you! (HE *raises his arms in the air, laughing.*)

I SAW MY DAD IN A DREAM

BY IAN DIMAPASOK

IAN, *a young boy 9-11, is living his life in the Philippines when* HE *receives terrible news.*

SCENE
The Philippines.

TIME
After arriving back from the United States.

IAN: I was at my house in the Philippines. I was just doing my chores and helping around the house. I said to myself, "Why do I have to do these stupid chores? How can it make me a better person? I hate chores." While I was finishing up, a guy came up to me. He gave me a letter. I opened the letter. (HE *opens the letter.*) It was from my sister, who was in the U.S. at that time. She wrote that I have to come there right away. So then someone bought a plane ticket for me and I landed in the U.S. two weeks later.

My sister was waiting for me at the airport. Then we went into her car and she asked me, "Do you know why you are here?" I said no, I didn't. She said, "You are here because our dad has passed away." When she said those words I didn't believe her. I started getting so mad that I was hitting everything in the car, including my sister. She told me to calm down, and that hitting her won't do me any good. When we got to her house she told me that we were going to have a funeral for our dad. I started crying like a little baby.... A few days later, we had a funeral for him. Everybody we knew was there. Everybody started crying like me. I was so sad that I fell asleep. Then I had a dream about my dad. He came back to life in my dream. He told me to keep on going with my life and don't be sad because he has a new life in heaven. After he told me that, he disappeared. After I had this dream, somebody woke me up. The guy said that the funeral was over. So then I went back to my sister's house and thought about my dream. I was happy that my dad was going to have a new life in heaven. Then I went back to the Philippines two weeks later. I haven't seen him again in my dreams, but I still think about him a lot.

IT'S NICE TO BE RICH

BY BRIANA DEAHL

MELODY, *12-14, rich, British accent, overdramatic, at her big birthday cake of a house, is having breakfast with her family when* SHE *learns some troubling news.*

SCENE
The dinner table at the family mansion in London.

TIME
Teatime.

MELODY: Pass the scones, please. Why, thank you. Oh, isn't it nice to be the richest family in London? Why did everyone cough when I said that? You must all be catching a cold. Wait…but now you're all looking at your plates? Something is wrong, can someone please tell me? Did another butler quit? That's not a big deal, we've got plenty more, and of course—What!? What do you mean by "poor"? Does that mean, like we're a couple billion short this month?—because I'll cut back on shopping if you want me to, I mean, I practically bought everything at every mall in England. No! This can't be happening! We can't sell this house, unless we buy one bigger and better. Don't tell me you can't afford it! Why did you get fired anyway? This is outrageous! I'm calling the government right now to get your company back up! They can't possibly fire the CEO of Google!

When do we have to be out of this house? One month! I can't pack up all of my rooms in that amount of time! I will just have to sit in my fourth room and lock the door. I am on protest! Do you hear me? Protest! (*To Butler.*) Butler, I'll have my caviar in my room. Oh, and bring me my stuffed bear, Mr. Ruggles. He's the only one who understands me.

KAGAMI'S TALE

BY JOSINE TORRES

Now a teenager, KAGAMI, *wearing a regular white shirt with blue capris, is kneeling on the floor.* SHE *is cutting out a newspaper article, addressing a boy named Yauso, a friend from her past.* KAGAMI *has returned to the home where* SHE *used to live before her parents died.*

SCENE
In an office in KAGAMI*'s house in Kobe, Japan. There is a desk and bookcases full of books. The door to the office is half open. A teenage boy named Yauso, in his school uniform, stands at the door. He seems to be staring at the girl.*

TIME
The present; late-afternoon sun.

KAGAMI: You know we have met before, but you don't remember. I thought that you would when you came to the library. I saw that same little boy, but you didn't remember me as a little girl. We met when we were six. I didn't have too many friends, but then one day you tumbled into my yard.... Two months later I invited you to my seventh birthday. You know all I wanted for my birthday was a big, fluffy teddy bear, since that's what little girls my age want. The week before that my parents had a meeting all the way in London, and they weren't able to come. They promised they would get me the fluffiest, biggest teddy bear there. I told them I hated them. The day of my birthday you didn't come and the maid was sick, so I was simply alone. That afternoon a man came, and he asked for my parents' papers, which discussed some type of invention. I shut the door and ran upstairs. When I turned on the television, the newscaster said that there was a big airplane crash near the coast of Kobe. They said…they said that that was the plane my parents took. There were zero survivors. On that day, I promised that I would be as smart as them. I'll be a good girl from now on and study really hard to make them proud. You know, I was never able to receive that bear, but I wonder where it is now, and if there is a letter with it from my parents.

THE SLACKER WOLF

BY ALEX JOVEL

Hey, everyone deserves their day in court, even the WOLF *from "The Three Little Pigs." As the teen* WOLF *tells it,* HE*'s just a victim of circumstances. Do you believe him?*

SCENE

A courtroom.

TIME

Right now.

WOLF: (*A* WOLF *in a wolf shirt and wolf shorts and no shoes.*) Yes, Judge, I am a wolf. I can't deny it. And why would I want to? You have to love yourself or you can't love anyone else, right? So I reject all those wolves who don't like being wolves. But I'm a loving wolf, Judge. And I think that officer made a terrible mistake when he arrested me.

(*In hippie voice.*) I mean, hey man, I'm a carnivore, a meat eater; you know? And I even had a really bad cold that day, man. I blew down their houses by accident. I had to eat the two pigs because I was really hungry.

Do any of you know what jail is like? Well, I don't. You should put that pig in prison or a mental hospital for being mean to a wolf. I'm young, with my whole life ahead of me. I'm gonna turn my whole life around after this, Judge. Yes, sir, I've learned my lesson.

Come on, Judge, you're a bear, you eat meaty fish.

(*In an angry voice.*) WHAT!? You find me guilty for what a lying pig told you instead of what an honest wolf said? I can't believe this is happening to me. I am going to prison.

(*Sobs.*) You people should find me not guilty. Instead of eating a buffet of pig, now I'm gonna be eating a small portion of chili in prison, cold, disgusting chili! (*Back to hippie voice.*) Hey, are you even serious about calling me guilty? I'm a laid-back wolf, Judge, I like everybody! I just want everyone to be happy, Judge, you know? Peace and love, my homies. I feel your pain, amigos! It takes a village!

(*In a crazy whisper.*) That pig is going to pay for what he did. I should have eaten him while I had the chance.... When I get out of my prison cell, I'm gonna go to that pig's stupid house and...get a flamethrower.... Things like that...I'm gonna go to that pig's house and...get a flamethrower...and ROAST THAT STUPID PIG! (*Back to hippie voice.*) Hey, it's all good, Judge, it's all good. You can't keep a good wolf down, you know? (*To Pig.*) And, hey, little Piggy, I'll see you in my dreams. If you know what I mean.... I'll be dreaming of my first meal when I walk...when I'm free. Maybe you can join me, wouldn't you like to do that? Peace out!

(HE *smiles, dancing out of the courtroom.*)

ZOMBIE ATTACK

BY MATTIE MOTZ

A zombie attack is going on in Burbank! Stay calm and stick close to MATTIE MOTZ*!*

SCENE

In the classroom at school in Burbank.

TIME

NOW!!!

MATTIE: I need to stay calm. It's not like the first time I've been in a zombie attack drill before. I've been in many. No, don't lie to yourself, Mattie. Lying only hurts your soul. I'm hurting my soul right now. But that doesn't matter. I might not even have a soul anymore after the zombies attack. But I'm ready.…I am going to make them wish they never even came alive again. Oh boy, Mrs. Cuseo is standing up to tell us an announcement about the zombies.… She's yelling, "Five minutes! They're going to attack in five minutes!" She's serious. There's actually a zombie attacking the school. (*In a calmer voice.*) You know the thing I said about attacking the zombies and making them wish they never came alive again? Well, I'm hurting my soul again. Don't tell me to stop talking to myself, Garret! (*In a little bit of a calmer tone of voice.*) I talk to myself when I'm nervous. I know, Leah, I have to be quiet so the zombies don't find out where we are. I get it. A call slip for me? I wonder who it's from. From Mom and Dad? (*Now* SHE *is paranoid.*) Maybe it's a trap. Maybe the zombies kidnapped my parents and forced them to write this call slip, tricking me into coming to their location. That's when they'll strap me down to their table and eat my brains out. (*In an angry voice, no longer paranoid.*) I know I'm talking to myself again, Garret!...I know I may be being a bit paranoid, I understand I might be a bit overdramatic....But there are zombies attacking Burbank, California! There's Mom and Dad. (SHE *waves to parents while saying "hi."*) Um, Mr. Lightfoot. Can I go to my parents? You know, so I don't get killed...by zombies. Thank you so much, Mr. Lightfoot. You're a great teacher. I...hope you survive....

PLAY SOURCES AND ACKNOWLEDGMENTS

Aesop, © 1919 by Rand McNally & Company. "The North Wind and the Sun."

Barrie, James Matthew, © 1928. *Peter Pan, or The Boy Who Would Not Grow Up*. Reprinted with the permission of Simon & Schuster, Inc. Copyright renewed 1956 by Lady Cynthia Asquith, Peter Llewelyn Davies, and Barclays Bank, Ltd.

Bragen, Andy, © 1997. *Formaldehyde*. All rights reserved. Reprinted by permission of the author. For inquiries, visit his website (www.andybragen.com).

Burton, B. J., © 2013. *Jake's Speech*. All rights reserved. Used by permission of the author. Direct all inquiries to the author at P.O. Box 445, Wayne, PA 19087-0445 or at bj_burton@hotmail.com.

Cagan, Kayla, © 2013. *Dog People*. All rights reserved. Used by permission of Kayla Cagan. Direct all inquiries to the author at kaylawriting@gmail.com.

Carroll, Lewis, 1871. "Jabberwocky" from *Through the Looking-Glass*.

Castellani, Catherine, © 2012. *The Permian Extinction*. All rights reserved. Used by permission. Direct inquiries to Anne Reingold, The Marton Agency, 1 Union Square, Suite 815, New York, NY 10003, and at anne@martonagency.com.

Cervantes, Miguel de, © 1885. *Don Quixote*. Translated by John Ormsby.

Croft, Sandra, © 2013. *Jason*. All rights reserved. Used by permission. Direct all inquiries to the author at sandra.m.croft@gmail.com.

Cruz, Nilo, © 2004. *Night Train to Bolina*. Reprinted by permission of the author. Inquiries should be directed to the Peregrine Whittlesey Agency, 345 East 80th St., New York, NY 10021. For inquiries regarding performance rights, please contact Dramatists Play Service, 440 Park Avenue South, New York, NY 10016, or at www.Dramatists.com.

Dahl, Nominee (Roald) and David Wood, © 2009. *Danny the Champion of the World*. All rights reserved. Reprinted by permission. Inquiries should be made to Casarotto Ramsay Ltd., Waverley House, 7-12 Noel Street, London, WIF 8GQ, UK.

Dawson, Dylan, © 2013. *Fred, Formerly*. All rights reserved. Reprinted by permission. Inquiries should be made to the author at dylandawson@gmail.com.

Deahl, Briana, © 2010. *It's Nice to Be Rich*. All rights reserved. Used by permission of the author. Direct inquiries for the author to rd41464@yahoo.com.

Devriendt, Alexander, © 2007. *Once and for All We're Gonna Tell You Who We Are So Shut Up and Listen*. Scenario and Text by Alexander Devriendt and Joeri Smet. Reprinted by permission. All rights reserved. Visit the Ontroerend Goed company Web site and direct inquiries to the author at www.ontroerendgoed.be.

Dimapasok, Ian, © 2010. *I Saw My Father in a Dream*. All rights reserved. Used by permission of Ian Dimapasok. Direct inquiries for the author to edimapasok@gmail.com.

Dubrawsky, Sofia, © 2013. *Shawna*. All rights reserved. Used by permission of the author. Direct all inquiries to Sofia Dubrawsky at ainosofia@aim.com or www.sofiadubrawsky.com.

Edan, Michael, © 2012. *Seeing the Invisible*. All rights reserved. Used by permission of the author. Direct all inquiries to Michael Edan at starbody@optonline.net.

Edan, Michael, © 2012. "Something Unexpected." All rights reserved. Excerpted from the unpublished play *Voices* by permission of Michael Edan. Direct all inquiries to the author at starbody@optonline.net.

Euripides, © 1958 by University of Chicago. *Iphigenia in Aulis*. Euripides, *Complete Greek Tragedies, Volume 4*, edited by David Grene and Richmond Lattimore. Excerpts from *Iphigenia in Aulis* translated by Charles R. Walker. All rights reserved. Reprinted by permission of University of Chicago Press.

Field, Arabella, ©2012. *Penny-Wise* reprinted by permission of the author. Direct inquiries to the author at ArabellaField@gmail.com.

Fife, Stephen, © 2009. *Silas*. All rights reserved. Used by permission of the author. Direct inquiries to Stephen Fife at stevelf99@gmail.com.

Gardner, Herb, and Irwin A. Cantor, Trustee, © 1961, 1962. *A Thousand Clowns*. Used by permission of Random House, Inc. Any third party use of this material, outside of this publication, is prohibited. Interested parties must apply directly to Random House, Inc. for permission.

Gaudreault, Jean-Rock, © 2000. *Matthew and Stephen*. Translated by Linda Gaboriau. All rights reserved. Reprinted by permission of the author. Inquiries should be made to him at jeanrockg@videotron.ca.

Gaudreault, Jean-Rock, © 2002. *Two Steps From the Stars.* Translated by Linda Gaboriau. All rights reserved. Reprinted by permission of the author. Inquiries should be made to him at jeanrockg@videotron.ca.

Graf, Wendy, © 2012. "In the Land of My Birth." Excerpted from the author's full-length one person play *No Word in Guyanese for Me.* All rights reserved. Used by permission of Wendy Graf. Direct inquiries to the author at WGraf89132@gmail.com.

Hackett, Albert, Frances Goodrich Hackett, and Otto Frank, Copyright, as an unpublished work, 1954; Copyright renewed, 1982, by Albert Hackett, Frances Goodrich Hackett, and Elfriede M. Frank; Copyright, as an unpublished work, 1956, by Albert Hackett and Frances Goodrich Hackett; Copyright renewed, 1984, by Albert Hackett; © 1956, by Albert Hackett, Frances Goodrich Hackett, and Otto Frank; © 1958, by Albert Hackett, Frances Goodrich Hackett, and Otto Frank (Acting Edition). *The Diary of Anne Frank.* Reprinted by permission. Inquiries should be made to: Abrams Artists Agency/Flora Roberts Agency, 275 7th Avenue, 26th Floor, New York, NY 10001; 646-461-9379; Attn: Sarah L. Douglas.

Hamilton, Carrie and Carol Burnett, © 2004 by Kalola Productions, Inc. *Hollywood Arms.* CAUTION: The monologue from *Hollywood Arms* included in this volume is reprinted by permission of the author and International Creative Management. The English language stock and amateur stage performance rights in this Play are controlled exclusively by Dramatists Play Service, Inc., 440 Park Avenue South, New York, NY 10016. No professional or nonprofessional performance of the Play may be given without obtaining, in advance, the written permission of Dramatists Play Service, Inc., and paying the requisite fee. Inquiries concerning all other rights should be addressed to International Creative Management, Inc., 730 Fifth Avenue, New York, NY 10019.

Hansberry, Lorraine, © 1969, 1971. Excerpts from *To Be Young, Gifted and Black.* Penguin, 1969. Used by permission of the Author's Estate. Adapted by Robert Nemiroff. All rights reserved.

Hernandez, Ashley, © 2010. *In the Rags of a Henchman.* All rights reserved. Used by permission of Ashley Hernandez. Direct inquiries for the author to matilde_h@sbcglobal.net.

Horovitz, Israel, © 1990. *Barking Sharks*. All rights reserved. Used by permission of the author. Direct inquiries to Bruce Miller, Washington Square Arts & Film, 310 Bowery, Second Floor, New York, NY 10012, and at Bmiller@washingtonsquarearts.com; 212-253-0333.

Horovitz, Israel, © 2010. *Inconsolable*. All rights reserved. Used by permission of the author. Direct inquiries to Bruce Miller, Washington Square Arts & Film, 310 Bowery, Second Floor, New York, NY 10012, and at Bmiller@washingtonsquarearts.com; 212-253-0333.

Horovitz, Israel, © 2007. *Unexpected Tenderness*. All rights reserved. Used by permission of the author. Direct inquiries to Bruce Miller, Washington Square Arts & Film, 310 Bowery, Second Floor, New York, NY 10012, and at Bmiller@washingtonsquarearts.com; 212-253-0333.

Hudes, Quiara Alegría, © 2007. *Yemaya's Belly*. All rights reserved. Direct all inquiries to John Buzzetti, WME, William Morris Endeavor Agency, 1325 Avenue of the Americas, New York, NY 10019, and at jbuzzetti@wmeentertainment.com; 212-903-1166.

Ibsen, Henrik, © 1918. *The Wild Duck*. Translated by Eleanor Marx Aveling. Boni and Liveright, Inc., Publishers, New York. Plays included in the volume: *The Wild Duck, The League of Youth, Rosmersholm*. This translation forms the basis for Hedvig's monologue herein, adapted by Bob Shuman.

Jovel, Alex, © 2010. *The Slacker Wolf*. All rights reserved. Used by permission of Alex Jovel. Direct inquiries to the author at ljovel24@gmail.com.

Joyce, James, © 1918 by B. W. Huebsch, New York. *Exiles*.

Joyce, James, © 1916. *A Portrait of the Artist as a Young Man*.

Kirkeby, Jennifer, © 2009. *Eyes Wide Open*. Based on material in the author's play *Eyes Wide Open*, published by Baker Plays. All rights reserved. Published by permission of Samuel French, Inc. Direct inquiries to Samuel French Inc., Attn: Lysna Marzani, Contracts Manager, 45 W. 25th St., New York, NY 10010; lmarzani@samuelfrench.com.

Lashof, Carol S., © 2010, 2013. *The Underprivileged Club*, adapted from *Gap*. Reprinted by permission. All rights reserved. Please direct inquiries to the author at clashlof@gmail.com.

Linhardt, Christina, © 2012. *Dad*. All rights reserved. Used by permission of the author. Direct inquiries to Christina Linhardt at linhardtprod@earthlink.net.

Loomer, Lisa, © 1998. *¡Bocón!* Reprinted by permission of the author. All rights reserved. Direct inquiries to Peter Hagan, Abrams Artists Agency, 275 7th Avenue, 26th Floor, New York, NY 10001, and at peter.hagan@abramsartny.com.

Ludwig, Ken, © 2007. *Treasure Island.* Based on *Treasure Island* by Robert Louis Stevenson. All rights reserved. Direct all inquiries to Jonathan Lomma, WME, William Morris Endeavor Agency, 1325 Avenue of the Americas, New York, NY 10019, and at JDL@wmeentertainment.com; 212-586-5100.

Margulies, Donald, © 1993. *The Loman Family Picnic.* All rights reserved. Used by permission. Direct all inquiries to Derek Zasky, WME, William Morris Endeavor Agency, 1325 Avenue of the Americas, New York, NY 10019, and at DSZ@wmeentertainment.com; 212-586-5100.

Master, Susan Rowan, © 2012. *Going Home.* This monologue and a companion stage play are both based on the author's novel *Summer Song.* All rights reserved. Used by permission of the author. Direct inquiries to her at susan@srmasters.com and www.srmasters.com.

McCullers, Carson, © 1951. *The Member of the Wedding.* All rights reserved. Reprinted by permission of New Directions Publishing Corp.

Motz, Mattie, © 2010. *Zombie Attack.* All rights reserved. Used by permission of the author. Direct inquiries for Mattie Motz to motzhouse@charter.net.

Oyamo (Charles F. Gordon), © 2006. *City in a Strait.* All rights reserved. Used by permission of the author. Direct inquiries to oyamo@umich.edu.

Renshaw, Annabel, © 2009. *I Am Julianne Frank.* All rights reserved. Used by permission of the author. Direct inquiries for the author to ginanbel@yahoo.com.

Rivera, José, © 1997. *Maricela de la Luz Lights the World.* Published by Broadway Play Publishing. Excerpts reprinted by permission of the author. All rights reserved. Direct inquiries to Jonathan Lomma, WME, William Morris Endeavor Agency, 1325 Avenue of the Americas, New York, NY 10019, and at JDL@wmeentertainment.com; 212-586-5100.

Rollins-Fife, Eloise and Stephen Fife, © 2013. *Amy's Super-Amazing Incredible Makeover.* All rights reserved. Used by permission of the authors. Direct inquiries to them at stevelf99@gmail.com.

Ross, Brenda, © 2013. "The Outcast." All rights reserved. Used by permission of the author. Excerpted from the unpublished book *Sela in Fairyland.* Direct inquiries to Brenda Ross at BrenRoss1313@gmail.com.

Rose, Tammy, © 2013. *The Robot Monologue.* All rights reserved. Used by permission of the author. Direct inquiries to Tammy Rose at tamavarose@gmail.com.

Roth, Sarah, © 2010. *The Hamster.* All rights reserved. Used by permission of Sarah Roth. Direct inquiries for the author to nicolefifi@sbcglobal.net.

Schindewolf, Connie, © 2012. *Boots.* All rights reserved. Used by permission of Connie Schindewolf. Direct inquiries to the author at www.connieschindewolf.webs.com or connieschindewolf@yahoo.com.

Shakespeare, William. *Hamlet.*

Shakespeare, William. *Henry V.*

Shakespeare, William. *King John.*

Shakespeare, William. *A Midsummer Night's Dream.*

Shakespeare, William. *Macbeth.*

Shakespeare, William. *Romeo and Juliet.*

Shuman, Bob, © 2013. *The Handicappers.* Reprinted by permission of the author. Please direct inquiries to Bob Shuman c/o Marit Literary Agency at bobjshuman@gmail.com. Visit Bob's theatre Web site, *Stage Voices*, at www.stagevoices.com.

Shuman, Marit E., © 2013. *Aria for a Saxophone.* All rights reserved. Used by permission. Direct inquiries to the author c/o Marit Literary Agency at bobjshuman@gmail.com.

Skillman, Crystal, © 2013. *Geek.* All rights reserved. Used by permission. Direct inquiries to crystalskillman@gmail.com.

Skillman, Crystal, © 2012. *New.* All rights reserved. Used by permission. Direct inquiries to crystalskillman@gmail.com.

Solano, Bernardo and Stephen Fife, © 2013. *Bad Dream.* All rights reserved. Used by permission of the authors. Direct inquiries to bsolano@sbcglobal.net or stevelf99@gmail.com.

Sophocles, © 1954 by University of Chicago. *Antigone.* Sophocles, *Greek Tragedies, Volume 1*, edited by David Grene and Richmond Lattimore. Excerpts from *Antigone* translated by Elizabeth Wyckoff. All rights reserved. Reprinted by permission of University of Chicago Press.

Stoppard, Tom, © 1993. *Arcadia.* Reprinted by permission of Faber and Faber, Inc., an affiliate of Farrar, Straus and Giroux, LLC.

Surkes, Nathan, © 2010. *The Burns*. All rights reserved. Used by permission of the author. Direct inquiries for Nathan Sulkes to his parents at 818-967-9907 or contact the editors at kidsapplause@gmail.com.

Svich, Caridad, © 2004, as a manuscript for a first workshop; 2008, as the text for the premiere. *12 Ophelias (A Play with Broken Songs)*. Reprinted by permission of the author. All rights reserved. Production inquiries to Caridad Svich at www.caridadsvich.com or to New Dramatists Alumni at newdramatists@newdramatists.org.

Swain, Bara, © 2011. *Black Sheep*. All rights reserved. Used by permission of the author. Direct inquiries to Bara Swain at BCSwain4@aol.com.

Torres, Josine, © 2010. *Kagami's Tale*. All rights reserved. Used by permission of the author. Direct inquiries for Josine Torres to josineanne@yahoo.com.

Twain, Mark, © 1885. *Adventures of Huckleberry Finn*.

Wagner, Jane, © 1994. *My Life So* Far. Excerpted from *Edith Ann: My Life So Far, as Told to Jane Wagner*. All rights reserved. Used by permission of the author. For production inquiries, contact Vivian Schneider, VLSESQ149@aol.com.

Wagner, Jane, and Lily Tomlin, © 1986. *The Search for Signs of Intelligent Life in the Universe*. All rights reserved. Used by permission of the authors. For production inquiries, contact Vivian Schneider, VLSESQ149@aol.com.

Wallace, Naomi, © 2009. *No Such Cold Thing*. All rights reserved. Used by permission of the author. Direct inquiries to Ron Gwiazda, Abrams Artists Agency, 275 7th Avenue, 26th Floor, New York, NY 10001, and at ron.gwiazda@abramsartny.com.

Wang, Lucy, © 2013. *My Superpower*. All rights reserved. Used by permission of the author. Direct inquiries to Lucy Wang at chickfillet@gmail.com.

Wang, Lucy, © 2013. *Pretty for an Asian Girl*. All rights reserved. Used by permission of the author. Direct inquiries to the author at chickfillet@gmail.com.

Weiss, Jeri, © 2012. *Lemonade*. All rights reserved. Used by permission of the author. Direct inquiries to Jeri Weiss at mail4jweiss@yahoo.com.

Wilson, Lanford, © 1966. *The Rimers of Eldritch*. All rights reserved. Used by permission. For performance information, contact Dramatists Play Service, 440 Park Avenue South, New York, NY 10016; www.dramatists.com.

Whitehorn, Chloe, © 2012. *My Choice*. All rights reserved. Used by permission of the author. Direct inquiries to chloe.whitehorn@gmail.com or www.chloewhitehorn.com.

Wood, Annie, © 2012. *A Good One*. All rights reserved. Used by permission of the author. Direct inquiries to her at www.anniewood.com.

Wood, David, © 1987. *The See-Saw Tree*. Reprinted by permission. All rights reserved. Inquiries should be made to Casarotto Ramsay Ltd., Waverley House, 7-12 Noel Street, London, WIF 8GQ, UK.

Wright, Craig, © 2010. *The Iliad*. Adapted from *The Iliad* by Homer, as translated by Robert Fagles and from *The Iliad*, as retold by Ian Strachan. All rights reserved. Used by permission. Direct inquiries to Beth Blickers, Abrams Artists Agency, 275 7th Avenue, 26th Floor, New York, NY 10001, and at beth.blickers@abramsartny.com.

Wyndham, Asher, © 2013. "Mini's Yard Sale." All rights reserved. Excerpted from the author's play, *Leaving Paradise Valley*. Used by permission of Asher Wyndham. Direct inquiries to the author at asherwyndham@yahoo.com.

Younger, Kelly, © 2012. *Off Compass*. All rights reserved. Used by permission of the author. Adapted from the author's full-length play, *Off Compass*. Direct all inquiries to Bruce Miller, Washington Square Arts & Film, 310 Bowery, Second Floor, New York, NY 10012, and at Bmiller@washingtonsquarearts.com; 212-253-0333.

Zindel, Paul, © 1971. *The Effect of Gamma Rays on Man-in-the-Moon Marigolds*. Used by permission of HarperCollins Publishers.

Additionally, the editors would like to thank the writers included in this volume, as well as Applause Theatre and Cinema Books, Bernard Addison, Adriana Aleshko, Kathy Antrim, Brenda Apreza, Ruben Becerra, Kathleen Bonner, Fred Bull and Tammy Byers, Burbank Unified School District, John Buzzetti, Perry C. Cartwright, Center Theatre Group, John Cerullo, Caitlin Charles, Emma Cheshire, Traci Cho, Bruce Cohen, College of Mount Saint Vincent, Kimberly Cottrell, Colleen Coyne, Sebastian Derry, Sarah L. Douglas, The Drama Book Shop, Dramatists Play Service, Tom Erhardt, Faber and Faber, Carol Flannery, Giselle Flores, Peggy Flynn, Kelsey Ford, Victoria Fox, David Gibbs, Edith Golub, Kevin Gonzalez, Pam Green, Peter Hagan, Joyce E. Henry, Shirley Herz, Jeff Holcombe, Harri Hurley, Donna Jacklosky, Rob Jacklosky, Rebecca Dunn Jaroff, John Adams Middle School, Kim Johnson, Marybeth Keating, Jason Knight, Lorraine Kornreich, Jane Kozinski, Gabriella Landay, Bob Lasko, Jonathan Lomma, Natalie Lopez, Eric Lupfer, Charlotte Madere, Aram Martirosyan, Lysna Marzani, Lisa and Stanley Mavrogianis, Cathryn McCarthy, Thomas McCormack, Eileen M. McElduff, Alex McPherson, Emily Meagher, Alyssa Mena, Edward Meyer, Reb Migletz, Valerie Millo, Jennifer Moen, Kassandra Montes de Oca, Christopher Naranjo, Jaime Nelson, Nancy Nelson and Randy Lanchner, New York Public Library (New York Public Library for the Performing Arts, Dorothy and Lewis B. Cullman Center, Schomburg Center for Research in Black Culture, Spuyten Duyvil Library), Craig Pospisil, Chris Regan, Mariah Reilley, Jesus Reyes, Fabio Rodriguez, Kristina Rolander, Valery Rosales, Kristin Rossi, Sam Rudy, Brandon Sanchez, Sandy Sawotka, Karen Schimmel, Vivian Schneider, Aaron Schwartzbord, the Shuman and Nolan families, Rita Battat Silverman and Steve Silverman, Sarah Smith, Eric Stein, Rick Stewart, Buddy Thomas, Thomas Starr King Middle School, Anne von Schwerdtner and her family, Barbara Smith, Frank Towne, Max Weisman, Phyllis Wender, Peregrine Whittlesey, Michael Williams, Maggie and Tom Worsdale, Kennedy Yerkes, David Zindel, and Steph Zou.

ABOUT THE EDITORS

Bob Shuman is the owner of the Marit Literary Agency and the Web site *Stage Voices* (www.stagevoices.com), which includes his theatre writing and criticism. Bob is a publisher—who worked for many years as an editor in trade books—playwright, college professor, author, Fellow of the Lark Theatre Company, and recipient of Hunter College's Irv Zarkower Award for excellence in playwriting. He has also been agent and an editor on three previous monologue and scene books for Applause (which have included his own dramatic writing). He has written songs for and acted in children's theatre and composed music for productions of Shakespeare's *As You Like It* and *Twelfth Night*; additionally, he was agent and one of the editors for *Acts of War: Iraq and Afghanistan in Seven Plays* from Northwestern University Press, and he coauthored *Simply Elegant Flowers with Michael George*. He holds an MFA from the Dramatic Writing Program at New York University's Tisch School of the Arts. Bob lives in New York City.

Stephen Fife founded and ran The Young Actors Workshop, directing kids 7–15 in original musicals he wrote for them, including *Charming* and *Young Forever* (which was also performed by teens in Tokyo). His evening of adult comedies, *This Is Not What I Ordered*, is published by Samuel French. His other plays include *Blue Kiss, Sizzle Sizzle, Savage World, Mickey's Home, The Battle of Light and Darkness*, and *Scattered Blossoms*. His adaptation of Sholem Asch's play *God of Vengeance* was produced by the Jewish Repertory Theatre in NYC, then later in Tel Aviv (in Hebrew) and in Atlanta, where it was directed by Joseph Chaikin. Steve wrote about this in his memoir *Best Revenge: How the Theater Saved My Life and Has Been Killing Me Ever Since* (CUNE Press). A graduate of Sarah Lawrence and Columbia's School of the Arts (MFA), Steve was the first literary manager for Primary Stages (NYC). He has written feature articles on theatre for the *New York Times, New Republic, Village Voice, New York Newsday*, and others. He also writes screenplays. Steve lives in Santa Monica, California.

Eloise Rollins-Fife started work on this project when she was a 13-year-old eighth grader at The Archer School for Girls. Her favorite things to do are sing, act, read, write, listen to music, and hang out with her friends. Her dream job would be as a writer/director.

Marit E. Shuman began work on this book when she was 14 years old. From New York, she attends The Horace Mann School. She is a lover of musical theatre and is a member of The Horace Mann Theatre Company, The Horace Mann Glee Club, and the Girl's Ensemble.

Other Monologue Books

Available from
Applause Books &
Limelight Editions

Duo!
The Best Scenes for Two
for the 21st Century

*edited by Joyce E. Henry,
Rebecca Dunn Jaroff, and Bob Shuman*
Foreword by Vivian Matalon
Applause Theatre & Cinema Books
9781557837028 .... $18.99

Duo!
Best Scenes for the 90's

*edited by John Horvath, Lavonne Mueller and
Jack Temchin*
Applause Theatre & Cinema Books
9781557830302 .... $18.99

The Monologue Audition
A Practical Guide for Actors

by Karen Kohlhaas
Limelight Editions
9780879102913 .... $19.99

One on One
The Best Men's Monologues
for the 21st Century

*edited by Joyce E. Henry, Rebecca Dunn Jaroff,
and Bob Shuman*
Applause Theatre & Cinema Books
9781557837011 .... $16.99

One on One
The Best Women's Monologues
for the 21st Century

*edited by Joyce E. Henry, Rebecca Dunn Jaroff,
and Bob Shuman*
Applause Theatre & Cinema Books
9781557837004 .... $18.99

Soliloquy!
The Shakespeare Monologues

edited by Michael Earley and Philippa Keil
Applause Theatre & Cinema Books
9780936839783 Men's Edition..................... $11.95
9780936839790 Women's Edition................ $14.95

Childsplay
A Collection of Scenes and Monologues
for Children

edited by Kerry Muir
Limelight Editions
9780879101886 .... $14.99

AN IMPRINT OF

Prices, contents, and availability subject to change without notice.

0213

More Acting Titles Available From

AN IMPRINT OF
HAL•LEONARD®

The Perfect Monologue
How to Find and Perform the Monologue That Will Get You the Part
by Ginger Howard Friedman
Limelight Editions
9780879103002 ....$16.99

Winning Auditions
101 Strategies for Actors
by Mark Brandon
Limelight Editions
9780879103163 ....$10.99

Monologue Mastery
How to Find and Perform the Perfect Monologue
by Prudence Wright Holmes
Limelight Editions
9780879103705 ....$14.99

The Monologue Workshop
from Search to Discovery in Audition and Performance
by Jack Poggi
Applause Theatre & Cinema Books
9781557830319 ....$16.99

The Monologue Audition
A Practical Guide for Actors
by Karen Kohlhaas
Limelight Editions
9780879102913 ....$19.99

The Scene Study Book
by Bruce Miller
Limelight Editions
9780879103712 ....$16.99

Acting Solo
by Bruce Miller
Limelight Editions
9780879103750 ....$16.99

Stella Adler – The Art of Acting
compiled & edited by Howard Kissel
Applause Theatre & Cinema Books
9781557833730 ....$27.00

Acting with Adler
by Joanna Rotté
Limelight Editions
9780879102982 ....$14.95

Accents
A Manual for Actors – Revised and Updated
by Robert Blumenfeld
Limelight Editions
9780879109677 ....$29.99

Acting with the Voice
The Art of Recording Books
by Robert Blumenfeld
Limelight Editions
9780879103019 ....$19.95

How to Rehearse When There Is No Rehearsal
Acting and the Media
by Alice Spivak with Robert Blumenfeld
Limelight Editions
9780879103422 ....$19.95

Getting the Part
Thirty-Three Professional Casting Directors Tell You How to Get Work in Theater, Films, and TV
by Judith Searle
Limelight Editions
9780879101947 ....$18.95

Prices, contents, and availability subjest to change without notice.

0213